Existentialism
Is a Humanism

Existentialism Is a Humanism

(L'Existentialisme est un humanisme)

JEAN-PAUL SARTRE

including A Commentary on *The Stranger*

(Explication de *L'Étranger*)

Translated by CAROL MACOMBER

Introduction by ANNIE COHEN-SOLAL

Notes and Preface by ARLETTE ELKAÏM-SARTRE

Edited by JOHN KULKA

YALE UNIVERSITY PRESS / NEW HAVEN & LONDON

Designed by Mary Valencia.
Set in Janson type by Keystone Typesetting, Inc.
Printed in the United States of America.

Library of Congress Cataloging-in-Publication Data
Sartre, Jean-Paul, 1905–1980.
[Existentialisme est un humanisme. English]
Existentialism is a humanism ; including, A commentary on the stranger /
Jean-Paul Sartre ; translated by Carol Macomber ; introduction by Annie
Cohen-Solal ; notes and preface by Arlette Elkaïm-Sartre.
p.   cm.
Includes bibliographical references and index.
ISBN 978-0-300-11546-8 (alk. paper)
1. Existentialism. 2. Camus, Albert, 1913–1960. Etranger. I. Macomber, Carol.
II. Elkaïm-Sartre, Arlette. III. Sartre, Jean-Paul, 1905–1980. Explication de
L'étranger. English. IV. Title.
B819.S32 2007
142'.78 — dc22
2007002684

A catalogue record for this book is available from the British Library.

11

Contents

Preface to the 1996 French Edition

ARLETTE ELKAÏM-SARTRE

"Existentialism Is a Humanism" is a stenographer's tran-
script, originally written in shorthand and scarcely altered by
Sartre, of a lecture he gave in Paris on Monday, October 29,
1945. He was invited to speak by the Club Maintenant,
which was founded during the Liberation by Jacques Calmy
and Marc Beigbeder to promote "literary and intellectual
discussion." The text of the lecture was published the following year by Éditions Nagel. Why was the author of *Being and
Nothingness* (1943) so determined to convince people of the
humanistic nature of his doctrine?

It should be remembered that the publication of the first
two volumes of *The Roads to Freedom* earlier the same year
had been marred by scandal. We need not delve into all the
reasons why these two novels, *The Age of Reason* and *The
Reprieve*, so shocked the conformists of the day. The main
character was perceived to be either spineless or cynical.

Sartre wrote, "I think what bothers people most about my characters is their lucidity. They know what they are, and that is what they choose to be." Without moorings and lacking confidence, his character Mathieu obviously has little in common with an epic figure or a positive hero; his sole asset in his obstinate search for a genuinely free life—echoed by the philosophical quest of *Being and Nothingness*—is his own particular brand of dry lucidity, which is also a source of anguish. What happens to him, or what he does, matters very little, for he has not yet begun to really live. What people did not fully grasp is that the first of these books merely set the stage for the intellectual and moral drama of an emerging consciousness not yet fully mature by the end of the second volume. The reason for this may be that these two novels—which, indeed, had their share of staunch defenders—were easier to read than the author's philosophical works, and that their publication had the effect of amplifying and distorting Sartrean existentialism.

The controversies surrounding Sartre's assertions were intensified and muddled by what we would call today a media circus—hype and misunderstanding met by open or latent hostility and priggishness. The result of it all was a quasi-mutual invasion: of the writer by a notoriety that dumbfounded him, and of the public by existentialism. Expressions taken out of context, such as "Hell is other people," "Existence precedes essence," or "Man is a useless passion," wandered into the tabloids and were bandied about like so many sinister slogans.

As for the criticisms voiced by intellectuals, who were not above casting insults, these were not yet based on a very thorough study of *Being and Nothingness*.[1] Christians chastised Sartre not only for his atheism but for being a materialist, while Communists reproached him for not being one. The former charged him with "arbitrarily making a cult of Being-in-itself"; the latter accused him of subjectivism. His ideas on contingency, abandonment, and anguish repelled both sides. Could it be that the violent expression of this rejection, which Sartre experienced as hatred, had everything to do with the fact that the nation — after the cataclysm of war — was (as one of his detractors put it) "preoccupied with defining man in accordance with historical contingencies, in a way that would allow man to overcome the current crisis"? In actuality, these objections were more often moral — even ultimately utilitarian — than purely philosophical. No one was that interested in a debate over how the ideas in his work were orchestrated, or in the relevance of his arguments. "Not everyone can read *Being and Nothingness*," wrote the same critic.[2] Nonetheless, in many people's minds, Sartre was becoming the anti-humanist par excellence: he demoralized the French at a time when France, lying in ruins, most needed hope.

It was therefore to present the public with a consistent and more accurate perspective on his philosophy that Sartre agreed to give the lecture reproduced here.[3] The event was attended by a large and overzealous crowd that pushed its way into the lecture hall, and Sartre was certain it included at least as many curious onlookers drawn by the nefarious reputation of existentialism and its author as listeners who had a sincere interest in philosophy. Disconcerted, he declared existentialism to be a doctrine strictly reserved for philosophers — even though he was about to make it more or less accessible to the general public. Beyond a public he understood poorly, he was addressing his remarks to the Communists, with whom he wished to establish a closer relationship. In fact, just a few months earlier, he had been writing in their underground newspapers, but now those ties were severed and their hostility seemed to be increasing with the growing popularity of existentialism.

It was not, however, theoretical reasoning that had led Sartre to seek a reconciliation. *Being and Nothingness*, a rigorously written and dense text, improperly understood and often distorted, had become something beyond his control, although he still assumed responsibility for it. He had been working on the book for years, composing it in a kind of solitary euphoria during a period of involuntary idleness brought about by the "phony war" of 1939–1940 and then by the year he spent in a German prisoner-of-war camp. But all of his intellectual energies bent on discovering a truth about the state of Being and man's purpose in the world did nothing to prevent the feeling of powerless under the Nazi occupation of France. If he aspired to collective action, it is because he felt the weight of history and acknowledged the importance of social matters.

In the same month as Sartre's lecture, October 1945, the first issue of *Les Temps modernes* appeared. The aim of this review, founded by Sartre, was to support the social and economic struggles of the Left—which was represented, primarily, by the "Party of Firing Squad Victims" (the name assumed by the French Communist Party)—and, through its columns, feature articles, and studies, to promote the liberation of mankind. Nonetheless, the editors of *Les Temps modernes* reserved the right to criticize: "We are siding with those who want to change both the social condition of mankind and its conception of itself. Furthermore, as far as future political and social events are concerned, our publication will take a position on a case-by-case basis. It will not do so *politically*, which means that it will not serve any party."[4]

This freedom of judgment was something the Communist Party's theorists wanted no part of; it "is playing into the hands of the reactionaries," was *L'Humanité*'s stock phrase for it.[5] The idea of freedom posed a problem on the theoretical plane as well. In his lecture, and at this point in his philosophical search, Sartre would have liked to be able to convince the Communist Party's Marxists that freedom did not contradict the Marxist idea that man is determined by his economic conditions. "A man who is free and one who is enslaved cannot be perceived from the same perspective," he protested in *Materialism and Revolution*, wherein he uninhibitedly expressed his differences of opinion with the Communists.[6]

After reading *Being and Nothingness*, critics insisted that he morally justify his commitment; worse still, they reached some rather negative moral conclusions that they then immediately reproached him with.[7] In the hope of dispelling such misconceptions, Sartre felt compelled in his lecture to simplify his own theories, stressing only those that people were likely to understand. In the process, he resorted to toning down the dramatic aspect of the indissoluble link between human reality and Being: his personal concept of anguish, for example, derived from Kierkegaard and Heidegger, is reduced here to the ethical anguish of a military leader sending troops into battle. This reconciliation effort would fail miserably: the Marxists refused to give in.

But had there really been a misunderstanding? Perhaps not, if we heed what Sartre's Marxist critic Pierre Naville said during the discussion that followed the lecture: "I choose to ignore any particular questions about philosophical technique."[8] It is not easy for a philosopher to carry on a dialog if the person he is talking with gives no credence to his doctrine while refusing to engage in philosophical discussion! Naville also wrote a review of the event that paid tribute to this vague discussion: "Pierre Naville pointed out the contradiction. . . . *Even more clearly than in denser discourses*, we can see here what distinguishes Marxism from existentialism and from any other philosophy."[9] In reality, Sartrean existentialism, which appealed to young people, was being refuted not so much for any of its theories but above all else to keep it from stirring up confusion and hesitation. "You are keeping people from joining our ranks," Roger Araudy told him; and Elsa Triolet said: "You are a philosopher, therefore an anti-Marxist." Indeed, if the Communist theorists felt that debating Marxism weakened the certitude indispensable to militants in order to fight (pointlessly, moreover, since Marxism contained all the truths necessary to change the world), then they had failed to grasp the substance of the philosophical approach that Sartre would reaffirm in 1948: "To seek Truth is to prefer Being above all else, even in a catastrophic form, simply because it *exists*."[10] Later, he endeavored to show that the existentialist concept of man that he proposed — expanded on, in the interim, in his biographical essays — is not, unlike Marxism, an excessive philosophy.[11]

In any case, it is hardly surprising that Sartre very soon regretted permitting the publication of "Existentialism Is a Humanism." Many have read this text and though it is often considered an adequate introduction to *Being and Nothingness*, it is not: the lecture is a clear but simplistic discourse that reflects the contradictions Sartre was struggling with in 1945. He passionately wanted to be involved in collective life alongside the Communist Party, which was bringing hope to millions of people in that first postwar year, when even the most radical social changes seemed possible; but this stance was not philosophically informed. Marxists hastily criticized his work without having read it, and there was the issue of accounting for Marx himself, whose work Sartre had not seriously studied; he had only just begun to formulate his thoughts on the social and historic dimension of man. Moreover, was phenomenological eidetics the right tool for thinking about collective existence? "One essential factor in philosophy is time," wrote Sartre in "Search for a Method." "A great deal of it is required to write a theoretical work." That particular year, he was caught at an inopportune moment.

"Existentialism Is a Humanism," timely though it was in many ways, reveals — to those familiar with Sartre's earlier literary and philosophical work — a turning point in the author's intellectual life. A new cycle of philosophical inquiry was about to begin. As yet muddled and hostile as criticisms of his work were (which he tried to answer in this lecture), they raised new philosophical questions that he would address in his *Critique of Dialectical Reason*, following an unhindered process of maturation evidenced, among other ways, in his posthumous works.

Existentialism Is a Humanism
and
A Commentary on *The Stranger*

Introduction

ANNIE COHEN-SOLAL

In 1943, when Jean-Paul Sartre's "A Commentary on *The Stranger*" appeared in *Les Cahiers du sud*, French writers stifled by Nazi censorship for the past three years were enduring one of the most difficult periods in their lives. "We had lost all our rights, beginning with our right to speak," explained Sartre. "Because Nazi venom had seeped into our very thoughts, every true thought was a victory."[1] Published in unoccupied France, *Les Cahiers du sud* escaped Nazi venom, and it was from within the circumscribed freedom of its pages that Sartre first saluted Camus.

Five years earlier, with the debut of *Nausea* and *The Wall and Other Stories* only months apart, Sartre made his own noted entry into the world of French literature. "Who is this new Jean-Paul?" André Gide asked, invoking praise like "splendor" and "masterpiece." Members of the old guard of French letters—Jean Cassou, Gabriel Marcel, Maurice

3

Blanchot—each in turn participated in the rite of greeting the newcomer. And from Algiers, the twenty-six-year-old journalist and playwright Albert Camus expressed his unconditional admiration for *Nausea;* he called it "philosophy put into images" and "the first novel by a writer . . . of limitless talent from whom we can expect everything." After reading *The Wall and Other Stories,* he further asserted: "A great writer always brings with him his world and his preaching. Sartre's preaching converts us to nothingness, but to lucidity as well. The image he immortalizes through his creations— that of a man sitting among the ruins of his life—expresses . . . the greatness and the truth of this work."[2]

But the unanimous acclaim did not last. A cooler response greeted Sartre's first sallies into literary criticism. Beginning in 1937, in twenty or so devastating articles, he set up his own pantheon, showering some writers with praise, demolishing others, rising up against the sadly outdated France of François Mauriac while celebrating the modernity of Dos Passos and Faulkner; this he did with mordant sayings like "God is not an artist; nor is Mr. Mauriac," and "I hold John Dos Passos to be the greatest writer of our time." For some, Sartre was an executioner; for others, a providential discoverer; for all concerned, in any event, he was the one critic in French letters whose judgment was absolute and inescapable. At twenty years of age, as a student at the École Nationale Supérieure, Sartre already stood apart from his peers for his maturity and the power of his own systematic thinking. A great fan of cinema, jazz, the American novel, and German phenomenology, he shattered the rigid framework of traditional university teaching and set off a few legendary scandals. Thanks to his vast learning and curiosity for everything new, Sartre's talent as a literary critic was established early on. A pioneer who ignored the boundaries between genres and cultures, he developed his tastes and judgments with supreme self-confidence.

When he encountered Camus's *The Stranger*, however, his intellectual machinery jammed. Disconcerted in the face of the novel's "ambiguity," he confesses his perplexity — a singular admission from a writer later described as a radical innovator and an all-encompassing thinker.[3] "Among the literary productions of its time," Sartre writes, "the novel was itself a stranger. It came to us from the other side of the horizon, the other side of the sea; it spoke to us of the sun in that bitter spring without coal." Sartre beckons the reader to enter his analysis of *The Stranger*, to proceed with him through the awkward, blind advances of his hypotheses and this first, hesitant encounter with Camus. How astonishing to watch unfold this early, open interaction between two postwar literary giants!

"What are we to make of this character?" "How can we convey the unthinkable and disorderly succession of present moments?" "What is this new technique?" "How are we to categorize this clear-cut work . . . so obvious once you have the key?" Sartre considers *The Stranger* unclassifiable; he examines it closely, observes it, analyzes it, prods it, and calls upon the amazing reserves of his own readings. And by recourse to Camus's *The Myth of Sisyphus* — that is, by using his own strong point, philosophy — Sartre at last manages to penetrate the work and suggest a way to decode it.[4]

Another successful strategy allows Sartre to place Camus in a literary tradition that includes Kafka, Dostoyevsky, Gide, Hemingway, Somerset Maugham, Nietzsche, and Kierkegaard — with whom Sartre elsewhere acknowledges his own kinship.[5] Little by little, Sartre's viewpoint in "A Commentary on *The Stranger*" becomes clear — literary and philosophical references, themes, the tensions he perceives in Camus's work, along with the deft enunciation of philosophy at the very heart of fiction, all echo the problems Sartre faced during the slow and painful elaboration of his own first novel, *Nausea*, five years earlier. Indeed, Sartre recognized in Camus a brother, a literary twin with whom he shared the same reasoning, the same pessimistic radicalism, the same rejection of mystical or moral values, the same technique of constructing fiction around a particular philosophical theme — the absurd for Camus; contingency for Sartre.

Already in his commentary on *The Stranger* we see him acting as a mediator between the literary past and present: so much of his critical work sets out to explain the genesis of the great French literary works of the nineteenth century (Baudelaire, Mallarmé, Flaubert); and the many prefaces he wrote

(to works by contemporaries like Jean Genet, Nathalie Sar-
raute, Roger Stéphane, Paul Nizan, Franz Fanon, Albert
Memmi, Aimé Césaire, Léopold Sédar Senghor) amount to a
kind of scorecard. He continued to champion Camus when,
reigning supreme, he carved out the literary landscape of his
era: "The contemporary novel — with American writers,
with Kafka, and with Camus in France — has found its style."
Introducing existentialist theater in the United States, Sartre
affirmed that "Camus's style in *Caligula* is . . . magnificently
sober and taut." And in an article on the new writers emerging from the French Resistance, he referred to Leiris, Cassou, and Malraux, and then went on to devote the rest of the
piece to Camus, because he represented the possibility of "a
new classicism in France."[6]

Pursuing his analysis of *The Stranger*, Sartre addresses and
sometimes lectures the reader, calling on him as a witness.
"The shock you felt when you first opened the book and
read, 'It occurred to me that anyway one more Sunday was
over, that Mama was buried now, that I would go back to
work and that, really, nothing had changed,' was intentional.
It was the result of your first encounter with the absurd."
Fascinated by Camus's talent, Sartre conducts a twenty-page
stylistic examination of the work: a precise, thorough, didactic, and luminous essay. "The sentences in *The Stranger* are
islands," he observes. "We tumble from sentence to sentence, from nothingness to nothingness. In order to emphasize the isolation of each sentence unit, Camus has chosen to

tell his story in the present perfect tense." At the end of his analysis, an exhausted and serene Sartre declares Camus's work a veritable tour de force. And in one of those brilliant, typically Sartrean formulations, he stabs at a definition of the work: "a short moralistic novel — one with ironic portraits and a hint of satire — a novel that, despite the influence of German existentialists and American novelists, ultimately remains reminiscent of a tale by Voltaire."

In June 1943, four months after the appearance of "A Commentary on *The Stranger*," Camus, recently arrived in Paris, introduced himself to Sartre at the première of Sartre's play *The Flies*. There ensued between the two men a remarkable friendship. Camus proposed to Sartre that he travel to the United States as a reporter for *Le Figaro* and *Combat*, in effect pushing Sartre into the real world, showing him a way to escape his teaching duties and allowing him to explore a country that since childhood had held for him powerful fantasies about modernity. But Sartre's trip to the United States in 1945 brought unexpected consequences: it resulted in Sartre's first commitment to the concrete, and gave birth to his calling as an ethical militant, which would find its expression in the postwar years and in the extraordinary undertaking of the journal *Les Temps modernes*.

Literature, philosophy, theater, literary criticism, journalism, politics, cinema: Sartre and Camus were involved in every intellectual sphere, at the same time and using similar means. But nothing really swayed their political positions or their convictions. Each followed his own path without influencing the other in the least. It was later, in the midst of the cold war, that their political divergences would surface, at first behind the scenes and then publicly, finally bursting into the open in the bitterest of public confrontations in 1952 during the Algerian war. It was a quarrel that brought to mind other famous duels of French literature: Corneille versus Racine, Voltaire versus Rousseau, Breton versus Aragon. Sartre, the writer from metropolitan France, became the apostle of anticolonialism and took a radical, global position as prophet of every third-world cause. Camus, the Algerian, withdrew into an attitude of consensus-seeking, developing his mythology of fraternity and reconciliation: Sartre, the well-to-do bourgeois, the arrogant holder of the *agrégation* in philosophy, against Camus, the autodidact, son of Catherine Sintès, cleaning woman. It was a bloody battle that only a single, small sentence hidden in the otherwise very laudatory "Commentary on *The Stranger*" had foreshadowed: "Camus seems to pride himself on quoting Jaspers, Heidegger, and Kierkegaard, whom he seems not always to have understood."

Change of scenery. A liberated Paris; two and a half years later. Sartre had just published *The Roads to Freedom* and launched *Les Temps modernes*. After years of censorship, as the French press began to come alive again, Sartre became simultaneously one of its key players and one of its least expected products. On Monday, October 29, 1945, at the invitation of the Club Maintenant, he delivered a lecture with the sufficiently daunting title "Existentialism Is a Humanism." Its content was extremely technical; nothing could have foretold its impact.

Sartre spoke without notes in front of a restless and packed room. He began by defending existentialism against its detractors — against Communists, who accused it of being "contemplative," "a luxury," a "bourgeois philosophy"; against Catholics, who condemned it "for emphasizing what is despicable about humanity, for exposing all that is sordid, suspicious, or base" — and he responded to their objections one by one. He then went on to map out existentialism's territory, defining it as a kind of "optimism," and a "doctrine of action," and man as someone who "first exists: he materializes in the world, encounters himself, and only afterward defines himself. . . . He will not be anything until later, and then he will be what he makes of himself. . . . Man is nothing other than his own project. He exists only to the extent that he realizes himself, therefore he is nothing more than the sum of his actions . . . responsible for what he is . . . free . . . condemned to be free . . . commit[ing] himself to life." After criticizing the theories of Marx, Heidegger, Kierkegaard, Descartes, and Kant, and after citing Gide, Racine, Proust, Stendhal, Cocteau, and Picasso, Sartre again astounds his audience by returning to those ideas that marked out his world vision and nourished his entire work: "responsibility," "project," "freedom," "action," "individual," "solitude."

This lecture became one of the mythical moments of the postwar era, the first media event of its time, giving rise to the "Sartre phenomenon." ("Existentialism Is a Humanism" was immortalized a few months later in Boris Vian's novel *Froth on the Daydream*, which describes "Jean-Sol Partre" clearing his path with an axe.) Already sensing during the lecture that his public image was moving beyond him, Sartre anticipates this media phenomenon: "In the past, philosophers were attacked only by other philosophers. The general public did not understand philosophy at all, nor did they care. These days, philosophy is shot down in the public square." "Celebrity, for me, equaled hatred," he explained shortly afterward.

In fact, in 1945, the influence of Sartre's thought would contribute to the making, and even the mythologizing, of the Saint Germain des Prés neighborhood, with its church tower, its square, and its cafés — of which Sartre rapidly became the intellectual embodiment. His literary endeavors followed a pyramidal structure, with philosophy occupying the summit and bringing legitimacy to the other six spheres of his influence: critical essays, lectures, plays, movies, novels, and journalism. Such a vast enterprise inevitably touched everyone, from the general public to the educated elite; little by little, his reach spread across the rest of Europe and the world.

If today we can state unequivocally that Sartre became, around 1960, the first global public intellectual, a few sentences from "Existentialism Is a Humanism" allow us to date the origin of his "universal" project to 1945: "Every project, however individual, has a universal value. Every project — even one belonging to a Chinese, an Indian, or an African — can be understood by a European. To say it can be understood means that the European of 1945, though his situation is different, must deal with his own limitations in the same way, and so can reinvent within himself the project undertaken by the Chinese, Indian, or black African. There is universality in every project, inasmuch as any man is capable of understanding any human project." In the context of a postwar France caught up in its recent past and haunted by the demons of its Nazi occupiers and its collaboration with them, such statements are doggedly subversive: indeed, from this period on, Sartre would follow the path of cultural interrelations, foresee the change in the balance of world power, predict the end of European imperialist legitimacy, and discern the emergence of postcolonial politics in a prophetic world vision that was radically different from that of the prewar era.

Here, then, we have Sartre, one of the most prolific writers of the twentieth century, presented in this American edition as a literary critic and philosopher-lecturer, and seen through two texts produced more than sixty years ago in very different historical contexts. The essays are strikingly dissimilar: "A Commentary on *The Stranger*," polished, intricate, inspired, finely written, even brilliant, and one of the rare instances when Sartre appears disconcerted, perplexed; "Existentialism Is a Humanism," on the other hand, a didactic and graceless transcription of a lecture given in the specific context of the postwar era, and in very polemical circumstances. Can we reduce Sartre to these two roles? On evidence of two short pieces produced some twenty months apart, can we account for an enormous body of work written over a period of more than sixty years? Yes, it's true these essays deal with literature and philosophy, the two poles Sartre traveled between his entire life. But what about Sartre the intellectual? The playwright? The editor of *Les Temps modernes*? The political activist and his disputes with the Communist Party? The prophet of the third world? The friend of Maoist groups? The brilliant writer of *The Words*? The man who refused the Nobel Prize in literature? The executive president of the Russell Tribunal? How can we account for all of Sartre? How can we summarize him in this small portion of his work? And, as we contemplate such a diverse career, what can these two documents, taken out of context, convey to us today?

Many readers find themselves disoriented by a writer whose protean work remains unfinished, and whose numerous ways of critically questioning everything escape traditional categories. Yet the different strands of Sartre's thinking, his various preoccupations, can be traced through his work from beginning to end: knowledge through exploration and adventure, the need to travel, passion for the modern and the new, interest in the culture of the other, the settling of scores with colonial France and imperialist America, as well as his interest in the Flaubertian France of the nineteenth century, with which he never ceased to struggle. With his all-out criticism of the nineteenth century, with his anchorage in the French tradition of the eighteenth century and the cosmopolitanism of Voltaire and Diderot, and with his finger on the pulse of issues that would be raised by the society to come, Sartre defies historical reference points.

Sartre's permanence resides above all else in his unequivocal subversiveness. One sees it on display already in his insolence at twenty — the scandalous student and dissident mentioned above — the man who would rebel against all forms of authority. In the 1950s, he declared himself the adversary of de Gaulle; in the 1960s, the adversary of the United States; in the 1970s, the protector of Maoist groups. Sartre's body of work is anything but a closed, satisfying, reassuring system of thought. It is located in a philosophy of lived experience, in an attitude of rebelliousness in complete accord with his theoretical model, in a stubborn irreverence, in a rejection of seriousness, and in a very keen ability to perceive new cultural trends.

In truth, all of Sartre — writer, philosopher, committed intellectual — is concentrated, compressed into these two short, prophetic works. Freed of their cultural and historical baggage, these essays speak powerfully to young Americans of the twenty-first century. Isn't he already connecting with them about the culture of interdependency, the universality of the individual project, the duty to act, the critical stance — Sartre, the eternal rebellious teenager, their contemporary? Let's give him the opportunity to address this new audience, who will surely then go on to discover *Nausea*, *The Words*, *The Wall and Other Stories*, *The Family Idiot*, *The Condemned of Altona*, *The Roads to Freedom*, and so many more of his writings. Let him act with them as he did with his own students, shocking many of them when he declared one day at the Sorbonne: "The only way to learn is to question."

Translated by ALYSON WATERS

Existentialism Is a Humanism

My purpose here is to defend existentialism against some charges that have been brought against it.

First, it has been blamed for encouraging people to remain in a state of quietism and despair. For if all solutions are barred, we have to regard any action in this world as futile, and so at last we arrive at a contemplative philosophy. And inasmuch as contemplation is a luxury, we are only espousing yet another kind of bourgeois philosophy. These are the main reproaches made by the Communists.

Others have condemned us for emphasizing what is despicable about humanity, for exposing all that is sordid, suspicious, or base, while ignoring beauty and the brighter side of human nature. For example, according to Miss Mercier, a Catholic critic, we have forgotten the innocence of a child's smile.

One group after another censures us for overlooking humanity's solidarity, and for considering man as an isolated being. This, contend the Communists, is primarily because we base our doctrine on pure subjectivity — that is, on the Cartesian *I think* — on the very moment in which man fully comprehends his isolation, rendering us incapable of re-establishing solidarity with those who exist outside of the self, and who are inaccessible to us through the *cogito*.

Christians, on the other hand, reproach us for denying the reality and validity of human enterprise, for inasmuch as we choose to ignore God's commandments and all values thought to be eternal, all that remains is the strictly gratuitous; everyone can do whatever he pleases and is incapable, from his own small vantage point, of finding fault with the points of view or actions of others.

It is these various charges that I want to address today, which is why I have entitled this brief discourse "Existentialism Is a Humanism." Many will be surprised by what I have to say here about humanism. We shall attempt to discover in what sense we understand it. In any case, let us begin by saying that what we mean by "existentialism" is a doctrine that makes human life possible and also affirms that every truth and every action imply an environment and a human subjectivity. It is public knowledge that the fundamental reproach brought against us is that we stress the dark side of human life. Recently someone told me about a lady who, whenever she inadvertently utters some vulgar expression in a moment of anger, excuses herself by saying: "I think I'm becoming an existentialist." So it would appear that existentialism is associated with something ugly, which is why some people call us naturalists. If we are, it is strange that we should frighten or shock people far more than naturalism per se frightens or offends them. Those who easily stomach a Zola novel like *The Earth* are sickened when they open an existentialist novel. Those who find solace in the wisdom of the people — which is a sad, depressing thing — find us even sadder. Yet, what could be more disillusioning than such sayings as "Charity begins at home," or even "Appoint a rogue and he'll do you damage, knock him down and he'll do you homage." We all know countless such popular sayings, all of which always point to the same thing: one should not try to fight against the establishment; one should not be more royalist than the king, or meddle in matters that exceed one's station in life; any action not in keeping with tradition is mere romanticism; any effort not based on proven experience is doomed; since experience shows that men are invariably inclined to do evil, there must be strict rules to restrain them, otherwise anarchy ensues. However, since it is the very same people who are forever spouting these dreary old proverbs — the ones who say "It is so human!" whenever some repugnant act is pointed out to them, the ones who are always harping on realistic litanies — who also accuse existentialism of being too gloomy, it makes me wonder if what they are really annoyed about is not its pessimism, but rather its optimism. For when all is said and done, could it be that what frightens them about the doctrine that I shall try to present to you here is that it offers man the possibility of individual choice? To verify this, we need to reconsider the whole issue on a strictly philosophical plane. What, then, is "existentialism"?

Most people who use this word would be at a loss to explain what it means. For now that it has become fashionable, people like to call this musician or that painter an "existentialist." A columnist in *Clartés* goes by the pen name "The Existentialist." Indeed, the word is being so loosely applied to so many things that it has come to mean nothing at all. It would appear that, for lack of an avant-garde doctrine analogous to surrealism, those who thrive on the latest scandal or fad have seized upon a philosophy that hardly suits their purpose. The truth is that of all doctrines, this is the least scandalous and the most austere: it is strictly intended for specialists and philosophers. Yet it can be easily defined. What complicates the matter is that there are two kinds of existentialists: on one hand, the Christians, among whom I would include Karl Jaspers and Gabriel Marcel, both professed Catholics; and, on the other, the atheistic existentialists, among whom we should place Heidegger, as well as the French existentialists and myself.[1] What they have in common is simply their belief that existence precedes essence; or, if you prefer, that subjectivity must be our point of departure. What exactly do we mean by that? If we consider a manufactured object, such as a book or a paper knife, we note that this object was produced by a craftsman who drew his inspiration from a concept: he referred both to the concept of what a paper knife is, and to a known production technique that is a part of that concept and is, by and large, a formula. The paper knife is thus both an object produced in a certain way and one that, on the other hand, serves a definite purpose. We cannot suppose that a man would produce a paper knife without knowing what purpose it would serve. Let us say, therefore, that the essence of the paper knife — that is, the sum of formulae and properties that enable it to be produced and defined — precedes its existence. Thus the presence before my eyes of that paper knife or book is determined. Here, then, we are viewing the world from a technical standpoint, whereby we can say "production precedes existence."

When we think of God the Creator, we usually conceive of him as a superlative artisan. Whatever doctrine we may be considering, say Descartes's or Leibniz's, we always agree that the will more or less follows understanding, or at the very least accompanies it, so that when God creates he knows exactly what he is creating. Thus the concept of man, in the mind of God, is comparable to the concept of the paper knife in the mind of the manufacturer: God produces man following certain techniques and a conception, just as the craftsman, following a definition and a technique, produces a paper knife. Thus each individual man is the realization of a certain concept within the divine intelligence. Eighteenth-century atheistic philosophers suppressed the idea of God, but not, for all that, the idea that essence precedes existence. We encounter this idea nearly everywhere: in the works of

Diderot, Voltaire, and even Kant. Man possesses a human nature; this "human nature," which is the concept of that which is human, is found in all men, which means that each man is a particular example of a universal concept — man. In Kant's works, this universality extends so far as to encompass forest dwellers — man in a state of nature — and the bourgeois, meaning that they all possess the same basic qualities. Here again, the essence of man precedes his historically primitive existence in nature.

Atheistic existentialism, which I represent, is more consistent. It states that if God does not exist, there is at least one being in whom existence precedes essence — a being whose existence comes before its essence, a being who exists before he can be defined by any concept of it. That being is man, or, as Heidegger put it, the human reality. What do we mean here by "existence precedes essence"? We mean that man first exists: he materializes in the world, encounters himself, and only afterward defines himself. If man as existentialists conceive of him cannot be defined, it is because to begin with he is nothing. He will not be anything until later, and then he will be what he makes of himself. Thus, there is no human nature since there is no God to conceive of it. Man is not only that which he conceives himself to be, but that which he wills himself to be, and since he conceives of himself only after he exists, just as he wills himself to be after being thrown into existence, man is nothing other than what he makes of himself. This is the first principle of existentialism.

It is also what is referred to as "subjectivity," the very word used as a reproach against us. But what do we mean by that, if not that man has more dignity than a stone or a table? What we mean to say is that man first exists; that is, that man primarily exists — that man is, before all else, something that projects itself into a future, and is conscious of doing so. Man is indeed a project that has a subjective existence, rather unlike that of a patch of moss, a spreading fungus, or a cauliflower. Prior to that projection of the self, nothing exists, not even in divine intelligence, and man shall attain existence only when he is what he projects himself to be — not what he would like to be. What we usually understand by "will" is a conscious decision that most of us take after we have made ourselves what we are. I may want to join a party, write a book, or get married — but all of that is only a manifestation of an earlier and more spontaneous choice than what is known as "will." If, however, existence truly does precede essence, man is responsible for what he is. Thus, the first effect of existentialism is to make every man conscious of what he is, and to make him solely responsible for his own existence. And when we say that man is responsible for himself, we do not mean that he is responsible only for his own individuality, but that he is responsible for all men.

The word "subjectivism" has two possible interpretations, and our opponents play with both of them, at our expense. Subjectivism means, on the one hand, the freedom of the individual subject to choose what he will be, and, on the other, man's inability to transcend human subjectivity. The fundamental meaning of existentialism resides in the latter. When we say that man chooses himself, not only do we mean that each of us must choose himself, but also that in choosing himself, he is choosing for all men. In fact, in creating the man each of us wills ourselves to be, there is not a single one of our actions that does not at the same time create an image of man as we think he ought to be. Choosing to be this or that is to affirm at the same time the value of what we choose, because we can never choose evil. We always choose the good, and nothing can be good for any of us unless it is good for all. If, moreover, existence precedes essence and we will to exist at the same time as we fashion our image, that image is valid for all and for our whole era. Our responsibility is thus much greater than we might have supposed, because it concerns all mankind. If I am a worker and I choose to join a Christian trade union rather than to become a Communist, and if, by that membership, I choose to signify that resignation is, after all, the most suitable solution for man, and that the kingdom of man is not on this earth, I am not committing myself alone — I am choosing to be resigned on behalf of all — consequently my action commits all mankind. Or, to use a more personal example, if I decide to marry and have children — granted such a marriage proceeds solely from my own circumstances, my passion, or my desire — I am nonetheless committing not only myself, but all of humanity, to the practice of monogamy. I am therefore responsible for

24

myself and for everyone else, and I am fashioning a certain image of man as I choose him to be. In choosing myself, I choose man.

This allows us to understand the meaning behind some rather lofty-sounding words such as "anguish," "abandonment," and "despair." As you are about to see, it is all quite simple. First, what do we mean by anguish? Existentialists like to say that man is in anguish. This is what they mean: a man who commits himself, and who realizes that he is not only the individual that he chooses to be, but also a legislator choosing at the same time what humanity as a whole should be, cannot help but be aware of his own full and profound responsibility. True, many people do not appear especially anguished, but we maintain that they are merely hiding their anguish or trying not to face it. Certainly, many believe that their actions involve no one but themselves, and were we to ask them, "But what if everyone acted that way?" they would shrug their shoulders and reply, "But everyone does *not* act that way." In truth, however, one should always ask oneself, "What would happen if everyone did what I am doing?" The only way to evade that disturbing thought is through some kind of bad faith. Someone who lies to himself and excuses himself by saying "Everyone does not act that way" is struggling with a bad conscience, for the act of lying implies attributing a universal value to lies.

Anguish can be seen even when concealed. This is the anguish Kierkegaard called the anguish of Abraham. You know the story: an angel orders Abraham to sacrifice his son. This would be okay provided it is really an angel who appears to him and says, "Thou, Abraham, shalt sacrifice thy son." But any sane person may wonder first whether it is truly an angel, and second, whether I am really Abraham. What proof do I have? There was once a mad woman suffering from hallucinations who claimed that people were phoning her and giving her orders. The doctor asked her, "But who exactly speaks to you?" She replied, "He says it is God." How did she actually know for certain that it was God? If an angel appears to me, what proof do I have that it is an angel? Or if I hear voices, what proof is there that they come from heaven and not from hell, or from my own subconscious, or some pathological condition? What proof is there that they are intended for me? What proof is there that I am the proper person to impose my conception of man on humanity? I will never find any proof at all, nor any convincing sign of it. If a voice speaks to me, it is always I who must decide whether or not this is the voice of an angel; if I regard a certain course of action as good, it is I who will choose to say that it is good, rather than bad. There is nothing to show that I am Abraham, and yet I am constantly compelled to perform exemplary deeds. Everything happens to every man as if the entire human race were staring at him and measuring itself by what he does. So every man ought to be asking himself, "Am I really a man who is entitled to act in such a way that the en-

tire human race should be measuring itself by my actions?"
And if he does not ask himself that, he masks his anguish.

The anguish we are concerned with is not the kind that
could lead to quietism or inaction. It is anguish pure and
simple, of the kind experienced by all who have borne re-
sponsibilities. For example, when a military leader takes it
upon himself to launch an attack and sends a number of men
to their deaths, he chooses to do so, and, ultimately, makes
that choice alone. Some orders may come from his superiors,
but their scope is so broad that he is obliged to interpret
them, and it is on his interpretation that the lives of ten,
fourteen, or twenty men depend. In making such a decision,
he is bound to feel some anguish. All leaders have experienced that anguish, but it does not prevent them from acting.
To the contrary, it is the very condition of their action, for
they first contemplate several options, and, in choosing one
of them, realize that its only value lies in the fact that it was
chosen. It is this kind of anguish that existentialism describes,
and as we shall see it can be made explicit through a sense of
direct responsibility toward the other men who will be affected by it. It is not a screen that separates us from action,
but a condition of action itself.

And when we speak of "abandonment" — one of Heidegger's favorite expressions — we merely mean to say that God
does not exist, and that we must bear the full consequences of
that assertion. Existentialists are strongly opposed to a cer-

tain type of secular morality that seeks to eliminate God as painlessly as possible. Around 1880, when some French professors attempted to formulate a secular morality, they expressed it more or less in these words: God is a useless and costly hypothesis, so we will do without it. However, if we are to have a morality, a civil society, and a law-abiding world, it is essential that certain values be taken seriously; they must have an *a priori* existence ascribed to them. It must be considered mandatory *a priori* for people to be honest, not to lie, not to beat their wives, to raise children, and so forth. We therefore will need to do a little more thinking on this subject in order to show that such values exist all the same, and that they are inscribed in an intelligible heaven, even though God does not exist. In other words — and I think this is the gist of everything that we in France call "radicalism" — nothing will have changed if God does not exist; we will encounter the same standards of honesty, progress, and humanism, and we will have turned God into an obsolete hypothesis that will die out quietly on its own.

Existentialists, on the other hand, find it extremely disturbing that God no longer exists, for along with his disappearance goes the possibility of finding values in an intelligible heaven. There could no longer be any *a priori* good, since there would be no infinite and perfect consciousness to conceive of it. Nowhere is it written that good exists, that we must be honest or must not lie, since we are on a plane shared only by men. Dostoyevsky once wrote: "If God does not exist, everything is permissible." This is the starting point of existentialism. Indeed, everything is permissible if God does not exist, and man is consequently abandoned, for he cannot find anything to rely on — neither within nor without. First, he finds there are no excuses. For if it is true that existence precedes essence, we can never explain our actions by reference to a given and immutable human nature. In other words, there is no determinism — man is free, man is freedom. If, however, God does not exist, we will encounter no values or orders that can legitimize our conduct. Thus, we have neither behind us, nor before us, in the luminous realm of values, any means of justification or excuse. We are left alone and without excuse. That is what I mean when I say that man is condemned to be free: condemned, because he did not create himself, yet nonetheless free, because once cast into the world, he is responsible for everything he does. Existentialists do not believe in the power of passion. They will never regard a great passion as a devastating torrent that inevitably compels man to commit certain acts and which, therefore, is an excuse. They think that man is responsible for his own passion. Neither do existentialists believe that man can find refuge in some given sign that will guide him on earth; they think that man interprets the sign as he pleases and that man is therefore without any support or help, condemned at all times to invent man. In an excellent article, Francis Ponge once wrote: "Man is the future of man."[2] This is absolutely true. However, if we were to interpret this to mean that such a future is inscribed in heaven, and that God knows what it is, that would be false, for then it would no longer even be a future. If, on the other hand, it means that whatever man may appear to be, there is a future waiting to be created — a virgin future — then the saying is true. But for now, we are abandoned.

To give you an example that will help you to better understand what we mean by abandonment, I will mention the case of one of my students, who sought me out under the following circumstances: his father had broken off with his mother and, moreover, was inclined to be a "collaborator." His older brother had been killed in the German offensive of 1940, and this young man, with primitive but noble feelings, wanted to avenge him. His mother, living alone with him and deeply hurt by the partial betrayal of his father and the death of her oldest son, found her only comfort in him. At the time, the young man had the choice of going to England to join the Free French Forces — which would mean abandoning his mother — or remaining by her side to help her go on with her life. He realized that his mother lived only for him and that his absence — perhaps his death — would plunge her into utter despair. He also realized that, ultimately, any action he might take on her behalf would provide the concrete benefit of helping her to live, while any action he might take to leave and fight would be of uncertain outcome and could disappear pointlessly like water in sand. For instance, in trying to reach England, he might pass through Spain and be detained there indefinitely in a camp; or after arriving in England or Algiers, he might be assigned to an office to do paperwork. He was therefore confronted by two totally different modes of action: one concrete and immediate, but directed toward only one individual; the other involving an infinitely vaster group — a national corps — yet more ambiguous for that very reason and which could be interrupted before being carried out. And, at the same time, he was vacillating between two kinds of morality: a morality motivated by sympathy and individual devotion, and another morality with a broader scope, but less likely to be fruitful. He had to choose between the two.

What could help him make that choice? The Christian doctrine? No. The Christian doctrine tells us we must be charitable, love our neighbor, sacrifice ourselves for others, choose the "narrow way," et cetera. But what is the narrow way? Whom should we love like a brother — the soldier or the mother? Which is the more useful aim — the vague one of fighting as part of a group, or the more concrete one of helping one particular person keep on living? Who can decide that *a priori*? No one. No code of ethics on record answers that question. Kantian morality instructs us to never treat another as a means, but always as an end. Very well; therefore, if I stay with my mother, I will treat her as an end, not as a means. But by the same token, I will be treating those who are fighting on my behalf as a means. Conversely, if I join those who are fighting, I will treat them as an end, and, in so doing, risk treating my mother as a means.

EXISTENTIALISM IS A HUMANISM

If values are vague and if they are always too broad in scope to apply to the specific and concrete case under consideration, we have no choice but to rely on our instincts. That is what this young man tried to do, and when I last saw him, he was saying: "All things considered, it is feelings that matter; I should choose what truly compels me to follow a certain path. If I feel that I love my mother enough to sacrifice everything else for her — my desire for vengeance, my desire for action, my desire for adventure — then I should stay by her side. If, to the contrary, I feel that my love for my mother is not strong enough, I should go." But how can we measure the strength of a feeling? What gave any value to the young man's feelings for his mother? Precisely the fact that he chose to stay with her. I may say that I love a friend well enough to sacrifice a certain sum of money for his sake, but I can claim that only if I have done so. I can say that I love my mother enough to stay by her side only if I actually stayed with her. The only way I can measure the strength of this affection is precisely by performing an action that confirms and defines it. However, since I am depending on this affection to justify my action, I find myself caught in a vicious circle.

Moreover, as Gide once pointed out, it is almost impossible to distinguish between playacting and true feelings. To decide that I love my mother and will stay with her, or to stay with her by putting on a charade, amount to the same thing. In other words, feelings are developed through the actions we take; therefore I cannot use them as guidelines for action.

This means that I shouldn't seek within myself some authentic state that will compel me to act, any more than I can expect any morality to provide the concepts that will enable me to act. You may say, "Well, he went to see a professor for advice." But if you consult a priest, for instance, it's you who has chosen to consult him, and you already know in your heart, more or less, what advice he is likely to give. In other words, to choose one's adviser is only another way to commit oneself. This is demonstrated by the fact that, if you are Christian, you will say "consult a priest." But there are collaborating priests, temporizing priests, and priests connected to the Resistance: which do you choose? Had this young man chosen to consult a priest connected to the Resistance, or a collaborating priest, he would have decided beforehand what kind of advice he was to receive. Therefore, in seeking me out, he knew what my answer would be, and there was only one answer I could give him: "You are free, so choose; in other words, invent. No general code of ethics can tell you what you ought to do; there are no signs in this world."

Catholics will reply: "But there *are* signs!" Be that as it may, it is I who chooses what those signs mean. When I was in a German prison camp, I met a rather remarkable man, who happened to be a Jesuit. This is how he came to join the order: he had experienced several frustrating setbacks in his life. His father died while he was still a child, leaving him in poverty, but he was awarded a scholarship to a religious institution where he was constantly reminded that he had been accepted only out of charity. He was subsequently denied a number of distinctions and honors that would have pleased any child. Then, when he was about eighteen years old, he had an unfortunate love affair that broke his heart. Finally, at the age of twenty-two, what should have been a trifle was actually the last straw: he flunked out of military training school. This young man had every right to believe he was a total failure. It was a sign — but a sign of what? He could have sought refuge in bitterness or despair. Instead — and it was very clever of him — he chose to take it as a sign that he was not destined for secular success, and that his achievements would be attained only in the realms of religion, sanctity, and faith. He saw in all of this a message from God, and so he joined the order. Who can doubt that the meaning of the sign was determined by him, and by him alone? We might have concluded something quite different from this set of reversals — for example, that he might have been better off training to be a carpenter or a revolutionary. He therefore bears the full responsibility for his interpretation of the sign. This is what "abandonment" implies: it is we, ourselves, who decide who we are to be. Such abandonment entails anguish.

As for "despair," it has a very simple meaning. It means that we must limit ourselves to reckoning only with those things that depend on our will, or on the set of probabilities that enable action. Whenever we desire something, there are always elements of probability. If I am counting on a visit from a friend who is traveling by train or trolley, then I assume that the train will arrive on time, or that the trolley will not derail. I operate within a realm of possibilities. But we credit such possibilities only to the strict extent that our action encompasses them. From the moment that the possibilities I am considering cease to be rigorously engaged by my action, I must no longer take interest in them, for no God or greater design can bend the world and its possibilities to my will. In the final analysis, when Descartes said "Conquer yourself rather than the world," he actually meant the same thing: we should act without hope. Marxists, with whom I have discussed this, reply: "Obviously, your action will be limited by your death; but you can rely on the help of others. You can count both on what others are doing elsewhere, in China, in Russia, to help you, and on what they will do later, that is, after your death, to carry on your work and bring it to fruition, which will be the revolution. What is more, you must rely on it; not to do so would be immoral."

My initial response to this is that I will always depend on my comrades-in-arms in the struggle, inasmuch as they are committed, as I am, to a definite common cause, in the solidarity of a party or a group that I can more or less control — that is to say, that I joined the group as a militant and so its every move is familiar to me. In that context, counting on the solidarity and will of this party is exactly like counting on the fact that the train will arrive on time, or that the trolley will not derail. But I cannot count on men whom I do not know based on faith in the goodness of humanity or in man's interest in society's welfare, given that man is free and there is no human nature in which I can place my trust. I do not know where the Russian Revolution might lead. I can admire it and hold it up as an example to the extent that it is clear, to date, that the proletariat plays a part in Russia that it has attained in no other nation. But I cannot assert that this Revolution will necessarily lead to the triumph of the proletariat; I must confine myself to what I can see. Nor can I be certain that comrades-in-arms will carry on my work after my death and bring it to completion, seeing that those men are free and will freely choose, tomorrow, what man is to become. Tomorrow, after my death, men may choose to impose fascism, while others may be cowardly or distraught enough to let them get away with it. Fascism will then become humanity's truth, and so much the worse for us. In reality, things will be what men have chosen them to be. Does that mean that I must resort to quietism? No. First, I must commit myself, and then act according to the old adage: "No hope is necessary to undertake anything." This does not mean that I cannot belong to a party, just that I should have no illusions and do whatever I can. For instance, if I were to ask myself: "Will collectivization ever be a reality?" I have no idea. All I know is that I will do everything in my power to make it happen. Beyond that, I cannot count on anything.

Quietism is the attitude of people who say: "Others can do what I cannot do." The doctrine that I am presenting to you is precisely the opposite of quietism, since it declares that reality exists only in action. It ventures even further than that, since it adds: "Man is nothing other than his own project. He exists only to the extent that he realizes himself, therefore he is nothing more than the sum of his actions, nothing more than his life." In view of this, we can clearly understand why our doctrine horrifies many people. For they often have no other way of putting up with their misery than to think: "Circumstances have been against me, I deserve a much better life than the one I have. Admittedly, I have never experienced a great love or extraordinary friendship, but that is because I never met a man or woman worthy of it; if I have written no great books, it is because I never had the leisure to do so; if I have had no children to whom I could devote myself, it is because I did not find a man with whom I could share my life. So I have within me a host of untried but perfectly viable abilities, inclinations, and possibilities that endow me with worthiness not evident from any examination of my past actions." In reality, however, for existentialists there is no love other than the deeds of love; no potential for love other than that which is manifested in loving. There is no genius other than that which is expressed in works of art; the genius of Proust resides in the totality of his works; the genius of Racine is found in the series of his tragedies, outside of which there is nothing. Why should we attribute to Racine the ability to write yet another tragedy when that is precisely what he did not do? In life, a man commits himself and draws his own portrait, outside of which there is nothing.

No doubt this thought may seem harsh to someone who has not made a success of his life. But on the other hand, it helps people to understand that reality alone counts, and that dreams, expectations, and hopes only serve to define a man as a broken dream, aborted hopes, and futile expectations; in other words, they define him negatively, not positively. Nonetheless, saying "You are nothing but your life" does not imply that the artist will be judged solely by his works of art, for a thousand other things also help to define him. What we mean to say is that a man is nothing but a series of enterprises, and that he is the sum, organization, and aggregate of the relations that constitute such enterprises.

In light of all this, what people reproach us for is not essentially our pessimism, but the sternness of our optimism. If people criticize our works of fiction, in which we describe characters who are spineless, weak, cowardly, and sometimes even frankly evil, it is not just because these characters are spineless, weak, cowardly, or evil. For if, like Zola, we were to blame their behavior on their heredity, or environmental influences, their society, or factors of an organic or psychological nature, people would be reassured and would say, "That is the way we are. No one can do anything about it." But when an existentialist describes a coward, he says that the coward is responsible for his own cowardice. He is not the way he is because he has a cowardly heart, lung, or brain. He is not like that as the result of his physiological makeup; he is like that because he has made himself a coward through his actions.

There is no such thing as a cowardly temperament; there are nervous temperaments, or "poor blood," as ordinary folks call it, or "rich temperaments," but just because a man has poor blood does not make him a coward, for what produces cowardice is the act of giving up, or giving in. A temperament is not an action; a coward is defined by the action he has taken. What people are obscurely feeling, and what horrifies them, is that the coward, as we present him, is guilty of his cowardice. People would prefer to be born a coward or be born a hero. One of the most frequent criticisms of *Roads to Freedom* may be expressed as follows: "Frankly, how can you make heroes out of people as spineless as this?" This objection is really quite comical, for it implies that people are born heroes. Essentially, that is what people would like to think. If you are born a coward, you need not let it concern you, for you will be a coward your whole life, regardless of what you do, through no fault of your own. If you are born a hero, you need not let it concern you either, for you will be a hero your whole life, and eat and drink like one. What the existentialist says is that the coward makes himself cowardly and the hero makes himself heroic; there is always the possibility that one day the coward may no longer be cowardly and the hero may cease to be a hero. What matters is the total commitment, but there is no one particular situation or action that fully commits you, one way or the other.

We have now, I think, dispensed with a number of charges brought against existentialism. You have seen that it cannot be considered a philosophy of quietism, since it defines man by his actions, nor can it be called a pessimistic description of man, for no doctrine is more optimistic, since it declares that man's destiny lies within himself. Nor is existentialism an attempt to discourage man from taking action, since it tells him that the only hope resides in his actions and that the only thing that allows him to live is action. Consequently we are dealing with a morality of action and commitment. Nevertheless, on the basis of a few wrongheaded notions, we are also charged with imprisoning man within his individual subjectivity. In this regard, too, we are exceedingly misunderstood. For strictly philosophical reasons, our point of departure is, indeed, the subjectivity of the individual — not because we are bourgeois, but because we seek to base our doctrine on truth, not on comforting theories full of hope but without any real foundation. As our point of departure there can be no other truth than this: *I think therefore I am.* This is the absolute truth of consciousness confronting itself. Any theory that considers man outside of this moment of self-awareness is, at the outset, a theory that suppresses the truth, for outside of this Cartesian *cogito*, all objects are merely probable, and a doctrine of probabilities not rooted in any truth crumbles into nothing. In order to define the probable, one must possess what is true. Therefore, in order for any truth to exist, there must first be an absolute truth. The latter is simple, easy to attain, and within everyone's reach: one need only seize it directly.

In the second place, this is the only theory that endows man with any dignity, and the only one that does not turn him into an object. The effect of any form of materialism is to treat all men — including oneself — as objects, which is to say as a set of predetermined reactions indistinguishable from the properties and phenomena that constitute, say, a table, a chair, or a stone. Our aim is exactly to establish the human kingdom as a set of values distinct from the material world. But the subjectivity that we thereby attain as a standard of truth is not strictly individual in nature, for we have demonstrated that it is not only oneself that one discovers in the *cogito*, but also the existence of others. Contrary to the philosophy of Descartes, or of Kant, when we say "I think," we each attain ourselves in the presence of the other, and we are just as certain of the other as we are of ourselves. Therefore, the man who becomes aware of himself directly in the *cogito* also perceives all others, and he does so as the condition of his own existence. He realizes that he cannot be anything (in the sense in which we say someone is spiritual, or cruel, or jealous) unless others acknowledge him as such. I cannot discover any truth whatsoever about myself except through the mediation of another. The other is essential to my existence, as well as to the knowledge I have of myself. Under these conditions, my intimate discovery of myself is at the same time a revelation of the other as a freedom that confronts my own and that cannot think or will without doing so for or against me. We are thus immediately thrust into a world that we may call "intersubjectivity." It is in this world that man decides what he is and what others are.

Furthermore, although it is impossible to find in every man a universal essence that could be said to comprise human nature, there is nonetheless a universal human *condition*. It is no accident that today's thinkers are more likely to speak of the condition of man rather than of his nature. By "condition" they refer, more or less clearly, to all limitations that *a priori* define man's fundamental situation in the universe. Historical situations vary: a man may be born a slave in a pagan society or a feudal lord or a member of the proletariat. What never varies is the necessity for him to be in the world, to work in it, to live out his life in it among others, and, eventually, to die in it. These limitations are neither subjective nor objective; rather they have an objective as well as a subjective dimension: objective, because they affect everyone and are evident everywhere; subjective because they are *experienced* and are meaningless if man does not experience them — that is to say, if man does not freely determine himself and his existence in relation to them. And, as diverse as man's projects may be, at least none of them seem wholly foreign to me since each presents itself as an attempt to surpass such limitations, to postpone, deny, or to come to terms with them. Consequently, every project, however individual, has a universal value. Every project — even one belonging to a Chinese, an Indian, or an African — can be understood by a

European. To say it can be understood means that the European of 1945, though his situation is different, must deal with his own limitations in the same way, and so can reinvent within himself the project undertaken by the Chinese, Indian, or black African. There is universality in every project, inasmuch as any man is capable of understanding any human project. This should not be taken to mean that a certain project defines man forever, but that it can be reinvented again and again. Given sufficient information, one can always find a way to understand an idiot, a child, a person from a so-called primitive culture, or a foreigner.

In this sense, we can claim that human universality exists, but it is not a given; it is in perpetual construction. In choosing myself, I construct universality; I construct it by understanding every other man's project, regardless of the era in which he lives. This absolute freedom of choice does not alter the relativity of each era. The fundamental aim of existentialism is to reveal the link between the absolute character of the free commitment, by which every man realizes himself in realizing a type of humanity — a commitment that is always understandable, by anyone in any era — and the relativity of the cultural ensemble that may result from such a choice. We must also note the relativity of Cartesianism and the absolute nature of the Cartesian commitment. In this sense, we can say, if you prefer, that every one of us creates the absolute by the act of breathing, eating, sleeping, or by behaving in any fashion at all. There is no difference between free being — being as a project, being as existence choosing its essence — and absolute being. Nor is there any difference between being as an absolute temporarily localized — that is, localized in history — and universally intelligible being.

This does not entirely refute the charge of subjectivism; in fact, that criticism is still being made in several ways. The most common instance is when people tell us, "So you can do whatever you like." This is expressed in various ways. First, they tax us with anarchy; then they say, "You cannot judge others, for there is no reason to prefer one project to another." Finally, they say, "Since all of your choices are arbitrary, you receive into one hand what you grant with the other." These three objections should not be taken too seriously. The first objection, that you can choose whatever you like, is simply incorrect. In one sense, choice is possible; what is impossible is not to choose. I can always choose, but I must also realize that, if I decide not to choose, that still constitutes a choice. This may seem a purely technical difference, but it is very important since it limits whim and caprice. Although it is true that in confronting any real situation, for example that I am capable of having sexual intercourse with a member of the opposite sex and of having children, I am obliged to choose an attitude toward the situation, and in any case I bear the responsibility of a choice that, in committing myself, also commits humanity as a whole. Even if no *a priori* value can influence my choice, the latter has nothing to do with caprice; and, if anyone thinks this is just another example of Gide's theory of the gratuitous act, he has failed to grasp the vast difference between our theory and Gide's. Gide does not know what a situation is; he acts merely by caprice. Our view, on the other hand, is that man finds himself in a complex social situation in which he himself is committed, and by his choices commits all mankind, and he cannot avoid choosing. He will choose to abstain from sex, or marry without having children, or marry and have children. Whatever he does, he cannot avoid bearing full responsibility for his situation. He must choose without reference to any preestablished values, but it would be unfair to tax him with capriciousness. Rather, let us say that moral choice is like constructing a work of art.

At this point, we need to digress a moment to make it clear that we are not espousing an aesthetic morality, for our adversaries have shown such bad faith that they even reproach us for that. I invoke the example of artistic endeavor solely as a means of comparison. Having said that, has anyone ever blamed an artist for not following rules of painting established *a priori*? Has anyone ever told an artist what sort of picture he should paint? It is obvious that there is no predefined picture to be made, and that the artist commits himself in painting his own picture, and that the picture that ought to be painted is precisely the one that he will have painted. As we all know, there are no aesthetic values *a priori*, but there are values that will subsequently be reflected in the coherence of the painting, in the relationship between the will to create and the finished work. No one can say what tomorrow's painting will look like; we cannot judge a painting until it is finished. What does that have to do with morality? We are in the same creative situation. We never speak of the gratuitousness of a work of art. When we discuss one of Picasso's paintings, we never say that it is gratuitous; we know full well that his composition became what it is while he was painting it, and that the body of his work is part and parcel of his life.

The same applies to the moral plane. What art and morality have in common is creation and invention. We cannot decide *a priori* what ought to be done. I believe I made that clear enough when discussing the case of the student who came to see me: regardless of whatever ethical system he might attempt to follow, whether Kantian or any other, none would offer any guidance. He was obliged to invent his own laws. Certainly we cannot claim that this young man — who chose to remain with his mother, taking as his guiding moral principles his feelings, individual action, and concrete charity (or who could have chosen sacrifice by going to England) — made a gratuitous choice. Man makes himself; he does not come into the world fully made, he makes himself by choosing his own morality, and his circumstances are such that he has no option other than to choose a morality. We can define man only in relation to his commitments. It is therefore ludicrous to blame us for the gratuitousness of our choices. In the second place, people tell us: "You cannot judge others."

46

In one sense this is true, in another not. It is true in the sense that whenever man chooses his commitment and his project in a totally sincere and lucid way, it is impossible for him to prefer another. It is also true in the sense that we do not believe in the idea of progress. Progress implies improvement, but man is always the same, confronting a situation that is forever changing, while choice always remains a choice in any situation. The moral dilemma has not changed from the days of the American Civil War, when many were forced to choose between taking sides for or against slavery, to our own time, when one is faced with the choice between the Popular Republican Movement [a Christian democratic party founded in 1944] and the Communists.

Nevertheless we can pass judgment, for as I said, we choose in the presence of others, and we choose ourselves in the presence of others. First, we may judge (and this may be a logical rather than a value judgment) that certain choices are based on error and others on truth. We may also judge a man when we assert that he is acting in bad faith. If we define man's situation as one of free choice, in which he has no recourse to excuses or outside aid, then any man who takes refuge behind his passions, any man who fabricates some deterministic theory, is operating in bad faith. One might object by saying: "But why shouldn't he choose bad faith?" My answer is that I do not pass moral judgment against him, but I call his bad faith an error. Here, we cannot avoid making a judgment of truth. Bad faith is obviously a lie because it is a dissimulation of man's full freedom of commitment. On the same grounds, I would say that I am also acting in bad faith if I declare that I am bound to uphold certain values, because it is a contradiction to embrace these values while at the same time affirming that I am bound by them. If someone were to ask me: "What if I want to be in bad faith?" I would reply, "There is no reason why you should not be, but I declare that you are, and that a strictly consistent attitude alone demonstrates good faith." What is more, I am able to bring a moral judgment to bear. When I affirm that freedom, under any concrete circumstance, can have no other aim than itself, and once a man realizes, in his state of abandonment, that it is he who imposes values, he can will but one thing: freedom as the foundation of all values.

That does not mean that he wills it in the abstract; it simply means that the ultimate significance of the actions of men of good faith is the quest of freedom in itself. A man who joins a communist or revolutionary group wills certain concrete aims that imply an abstract will to freedom, yet that freedom must always be exercised in a concrete manner. We will freedom for freedom's sake through our individual circumstances. And in thus willing freedom, we discover that it depends entirely on the freedom of others, and that the freedom of others depends on our own. Of course, freedom as the definition of man does not depend on others, but as soon as there is commitment, I am obliged to will the freedom of others at the same time as I will my own. I cannot set my own freedom as a goal without also setting the freedom of others as a goal. Consequently, when, operating on the level of complete authenticity, I have acknowledged that existence precedes essence, and that man is a free being who, under any circumstances, can only ever will his freedom, I have at the same time acknowledged that I must will the freedom of others. Therefore, in the name of this will to freedom, implied by freedom itself, I can pass judgment on those who seek to conceal from themselves the complete arbitrariness of their existence, and their total freedom. Those who conceal from themselves this total freedom, under the guise of solemnity, or by making determinist excuses, I will call cowards. Others, who try to prove their existence is necessary, when man's appearance on earth is merely contingent, I will call bastards. But whether cowards or bastards, they can be judged only on the grounds of strict authenticity. Thus, although the content of morality may vary, a certain form of that morality is universal. Kant states that freedom wills itself and the freedom of others. Agreed. But he believes that the formal and the universal are adequate to constitute a morality. We, to the contrary, believe that principles that are too abstract fail to define action. Consider again the case of the student: in the name of what — what inviolable moral maxim — could he possibly have decided, with perfect peace of mind, whether he should abandon or remain with his mother? There is no way of judging. The content is always specific; inventiveness is always part of the process. The only thing that counts is whether or not invention is made in the name of freedom.

Consider, for example, the following two cases and you will see to what extent they are similar, despite their obvious differences. Take George Eliot's novel *The Mill on the Floss*. In that story, we encounter a young woman, Maggie Tulliver, who is the very incarnation of passion and is aware of the fact. She falls in love with a young man, Stephen, who is already engaged to a very ordinary young girl. Instead of recklessly pursuing her own happiness, Maggie chooses, in the name of human solidarity, self-sacrifice, giving up the man she loves. On the other hand, in Stendhal's *The Charterhouse of Parma*, La Sanseverina, who believes that passion is the measure of man, would say that a great love justifies any sacrifice, and must be preferred to the banality of a conjugal love like the one that would bind Stephen to his silly goose of a fiancée. It is the latter she would have chosen to sacrifice for her own happiness and, as Stendhal shows, she is even willing to make the ultimate sacrifice for passion's sake if life demands it. Here, we confront two diametrically opposed moralities, yet I maintain they are equivalent, inasmuch as the ultimate aim in both cases is freedom. Let us now imagine two different attitudes with strikingly similar effects: one girl, out of resignation, prefers to give up her lover, while the other, to fulfill her sexual desires, prefers to overlook the previous engagement of the man she loves. On the surface both cases seem to mirror those we have just described. However, they are completely different. La Sanseverina's attitude has more in common with Maggie Tulliver's than it does with careless greed.

So, you can see that this second objection is both true and false. One can choose anything, so long as it involves free commitment.

The third objection, which we said can be stated as "You receive into one hand what you grant with the other," means, at bottom, our values need not be taken very seriously, since we choose them ourselves. In response, I can say that I very much regret it should be so, but if I have eliminated God the Father, there has to be someone to invent values. Things must be accepted as they are. What is more, to say that we invent values means neither more nor less than this: life has no meaning *a priori*. Life itself is nothing until it is lived, it is we who give it meaning, and value is nothing more than the meaning that we give it. You can see, then, that it is possible to create a human community. Some have blamed me for postulating that existentialism is a form of humanism.[3] People have said to me, "But in *Nausea* you wrote that humanists are wrong; you even ridiculed a certain type of humanism, so why are you reversing your opinion now?" Actually, the word "humanism" has two very different meanings. By "humanism" we might mean a theory that takes man as an end and as the supreme value. For example, in his story *Around the World in 80 Hours*, Cocteau gives expression to this idea when one of his characters, flying over some mountains in a plane, proclaims: "Man is amazing!" This means: even though I myself may never have built a plane, I nevertheless still benefit from the plane's invention and, as a man, I should consider myself responsible for, and honored by, what certain other men have achieved. This presupposes that we can assign a value to man based on the most admirable deeds of certain men. But that kind of humanism is absurd, for only a dog or a horse would be in a position to form an overall judgment about man and declare that he is amazing, which animals scarcely seem likely to do — at least, as far as I know. Nor is it acceptable that a man should pronounce judgment on mankind. Existentialism dispenses with any judgment of this sort: existentialism will never consider man as an end, because man is constantly in the making. And we have no right to believe that humanity is something we could worship, in the manner of Auguste Comte. The cult of humanity leads ultimately to an insular Comteian humanism and — this needs to be said — to Fascism. We do *not* want that type of humanism.

But there is another meaning to the word "humanism." It is basically this: man is always outside of himself, and it is in projecting and losing himself beyond himself that man is realized; and, on the other hand, it is in pursuing transcendent goals that he is able to exist. Since man is this transcendence, and grasps objects only in relation to such transcendence, he is himself the core and focus of this transcendence. The only universe that exists is the human one — the universe of human subjectivity. This link between transcendence as constitutive of man (not in the sense that God is transcendent, but in the sense that man passes beyond himself) and subjectivity (in the sense that man is not an island unto himself but always present in a human universe) is what we call "existentialist humanism." This is humanism because we remind man that there is no legislator other than himself and that he must, in his abandoned state, make his own choices, and also because we show that it is not by turning inward, but by constantly seeking a goal outside of himself in the form of liberation, or of some special achievement, that man will realize himself as truly human.

From these few comments, it is evident that nothing is more unjust than the objections people have brought against us. Existentialism is merely an attempt to draw all of the conclusions inferred by a consistently atheistic point of view. Its purpose is not at all to plunge mankind into despair. But if we label any attitude of unbelief "despair," as Christians do, then our notion of despair is vastly different from its original meaning.

Existentialism is not so much an atheism in the sense that it would exhaust itself attempting to demonstrate the nonexistence of God; rather, it affirms that even if God were to exist, it would make no difference — that is our point of view. It is not that we believe that God exists, but we think that the real problem is not one of his existence; what man needs is to rediscover himself and to comprehend that nothing can save him from himself, not even valid proof of the existence of

God. In this sense, existentialism is optimistic. It is a doctrine of action, and it is only in bad faith — in confusing their own despair with ours — that Christians are able to assert that we are "without hope."

POST-LECTURE DISCUSSION

This discussion took place during the question-and-answer exchange following Sartre's lecture on existentialism. The first series of questions came from an unidentified member of the audience. Pierre Naville was a French surrealist author and leftist.

QUESTION: I don't know if this current effort to explain existentialism will make you better or less well understood, but I think that the clarification in *Action* makes your position somewhat harder to understand.[4] "Despair" and "abandonment" have an even greater resonance in an existentialist text than they usually do. And it seems to me that your understanding of "despair" or "anguish" is something more fundamental than a simple choice made by a man who realizes that he is alone and so must make his own choices. It is an awareness of the human condition that does not occur all the time. That we must choose ourselves at all times is evident, but anguish and despair are hardly common emotions.

SARTRE: Obviously, I do not mean that when I choose between a cream pastry and a chocolate éclair, I am choosing in anguish. The anguish is constant in the sense that my initial choice is a constant thing. Indeed, in my opinion, anguish is the total absence of justification accompanied, at the same time, by responsibility toward all.

QUESTION: I was speaking about the clarification offered in *Action*, and it seems to me that your viewpoint, as it was expressed there, was slightly weakened.

SARTRE: In all sincerity, it is possible that the article in *Action* did somewhat dilute my arguments. Many of the people who interview me are not qualified to do so. This leaves me with two alternatives: refuse to answer their questions, or agree to allow discussion to take place on a simplified level. I chose the second because, when all is said and done, whenever we present our theories in the classroom, we agree to dilute our thinking in order to make it understood, and that doesn't seem like such a bad thing. If we have a theory of commitment, we must be committed to the very end. If existentialist philosophy is, first and foremost, a philosophy that says "existence precedes essence," it must be experienced if it is to be sincere. To live as an existentialist means to accept the consequences of this doctrine and not merely to impose it on others in books. If you truly want this philosophy to be a commitment, you have an obligation to make it comprehensible to those who are discussing it on a political or moral plane.

I am reproached for using the word "humanism." That is because the problem poses itself as follows: either we must convey the doctrine on a strictly philosophical plane and then leave it to luck as to whether or not it will have any impact, or — since people are asking something else from it, and since it is intended to be a commitment — we must agree to popularize it on the condition that we don't deform it.

QUESTION: Those who want to understand will do so, and those who don't want to understand won't.

SARTRE: You seem to conceive the role of philosophy in the polity in an outmoded way. In the past, philosophers were attacked only by other philosophers. The general public did not understand philosophy at all, nor did they care. These days, philosophy is shot down in the public square. Marx himself never stopped trying to popularize his thought; the *Communist Manifesto* represents the popularization of his thinking.

QUESTION: Marx's initial choice was a revolutionary one.

SARTRE: Anyone who could say whether Marx first chose to be a revolutionary and then a philosopher — or first chose philosophy and then became a revolutionary — would be clever, indeed. He is a philosopher *and* a revolutionary: the two things are inseparable. He first chose to be a revolutionary — what can that possibly mean?

QUESTION: I do not consider the *Communist Manifesto* a popularization, but a combat weapon. I cannot imagine that writing it was not an act of commitment.

Once Marx the philosopher concluded that revolution was necessary, his first action was to write his *Communist*

Manifesto, which was a political act. The *Communist Manifesto* is the link between Marx's philosophy and Communism. Whatever your morality may be, it isn't likely to have the kind of close, logical connection to your philosophy as the one that exists between the *Communist Manifesto* and Marx's philosophy.

SARTRE: We are dealing with a freedom-based philosophy. If there is no contradiction between our morality and our philosophy, we cannot wish for anything more. The types of commitment differ in accordance with the times. In an era when an act of commitment was perceived as revolutionary, writing the *Manifesto* was a necessity. In an era such as ours, when various parties are each calling for revolution, making a commitment does not mean joining one of them, but trying to clarify concepts in order to both identify respective positions and attempt to influence the various revolutionary parties.

PIERRE NAVILLE: The question that we ought to be asking ourselves, based on the viewpoints that you have just expressed, is whether or not your doctrine is not going to be perceived (in the period to come) as a revival of radical socialism. That may seem strange, but it is the way in which this question should be asked. As a matter of fact, you are taking a position open to all sorts of perspectives. But if we were to look for a point of convergence between these various viewpoints and all these facets of existentialist ideas, I suspect that we would discover it was some kind of revival of liberalism.

Your philosophy attempts to revive — under very special conditions, that is to say, our current historical conditions — what once constituted the essential tenets of radical socialism and humanist liberalism. What makes the current situation different is the fact that the world's social crisis no longer permits the old liberalism; it demands a tormented and anguished form of liberalism. I think that we can probably isolate a number of rather profound explanations for this belief, even if we limit ourselves to your own terms. Your presentation makes clear that existentialism should be seen as a humanism and a freedom-based philosophy that is essentially a precommitment, a project that cannot be defined. Like many other people, you stress the dignity of mankind and the eminent dignity of the individual — themes which, by and large, are not so distant from old liberal themes. To justify them, you distinguish between the two meanings of humanism, between the two meanings of humanity, between the two meanings of the "human condition," and between the two meanings of a number of outdated terms that also have a significant history, and whose ambiguous nature is not coincidental. To justify them, you endow them with a new meaning. I will not be discussing all the special questions dealing with philosophical technique — despite their interest and importance — and will focus instead on the terms that I have heard. I will stress a fundamental point which shows that, despite the fact you distinguish two meanings of "humanism," you basically cling to the original one.

Man is defined as the choices he must make. Very well. Above all else, he exists in the present moment, and beyond natural determinism; he does not define himself prior to his existence, but does so according to his individual present. There is no human nature superior to his, but he is endowed with a specific existence at a particular moment. I wonder whether existence, understood in these terms, is not yet another form of the concept of human nature that has taken on a new expression for historical reasons, and whether it is not very similar — more so than it may seem at first glance — to human nature as it was defined in the eighteenth century, and whose concept you say you reject because traces of it can be found, to a large extent, behind the expression "the human condition," employed by existentialists. Your conception of the human condition is a substitute for human nature, just as you substitute real-life experience for common or scientific experience.

If we consider human conditions as those defined by "X," in which "X" is the subject, rather than by their natural context, or by their affirmative determination, we are confronting another form of human nature — a "nature-condition," if you will, meaning that it is not simply defined as an abstract type of nature, but manifests itself through something much more difficult to formulate, for what I consider historical reasons. Today, human nature is defined in social contexts characterized by a general breakdown of the social system, by classes, by conflicts that the latter experience, and by an intermixing of races and nations, as a result of which the very idea of a uniform and schematic human nature can no longer be perceived as having the same general character, or the same type of universality as it did in the eighteenth century — in an era that seemed to express itself in terms of continuous progress. In our own time, we confront an expression of human nature that thinkers, or those who speak naively about this issue, call "the human condition." They express this chaotically, vaguely, and most frequently in some dramatic fashion, if you will, dictated by the circumstances. And, to the extent that people prefer not to exchange the broad term for this condition for the determinist assessment of what conditions really are, they retain the type and outline of an abstract expression analogous to that of human nature.

Thus, existentialism clings to the idea of a human nature, but in this case it is not a self-congratulatory nature, but rather a fearful, uncertain, and forlorn condition. Indeed, when existentialism speaks of the human condition, it means a condition that is not yet truly committed to what existentialism calls "projects," and which is therefore a precondition. This calls for a precommitment, not a commitment or a true condition. Consequently, it is also no accident that this condition is predominantly defined by its overall humanistic nature. Moreover, in the past, when people spoke of human nature, they were referring to something narrower in scope than a general condition. After all, nature is already something else — to some extent it is more than a condition.

Human nature is not a modality in the same sense as the human condition is a modality. This is why I feel it is preferable to speak of "naturalism" rather than of "humanism." "Naturalism" implies broader realities than humanism — at least in the sense that people in your circles use the term "humanism." What we are concerned with is a reality. In fact, we should expand this discussion on human nature, for we also need to bring into play the historical perspective. The primary reality is natural reality, of which human reality is but a function. But in order to do that, we must first accept the truth of history, and existentialism does not generally accept the truth of history any more than it does human history or natural history as a rule. Yet it is history that shapes individuals; it is their own history, from the moment of conception, that accounts for the fact that individuals are not born into, and do not appear in, a world that provides them with an abstract condition, but they appear in a world they have always been a part of, which conditions them, and which they in turn condition, just as the mother conditions her child, and her child also conditions her, from the moment she becomes pregnant. Only from this perspective are we entitled to speak of the human condition as a primary reality. It would be more accurate to say that the primary reality is a natural condition, and not a human condition. In this, I'm only repeating common and ordinary opinions, but ones that I consider in no way refuted by existentialist theory. In short, if it is true that there is no such thing as an abstract human nature — an essence separate from, or preceding, his existence — it is also certain that there is no such thing as a human condition in general, even if, by "condition," you mean a number of real-life circumstances or situations because, in your opinion, they have not been articulated. In any event, Marxism has a different conception of this matter — that of nature in man and of man in nature — that is not necessarily defined from an individual viewpoint.

This means that there are laws that operate for man just as there are for any other object of scientific inquiry. These laws constitute, in the deepest sense of the term, his nature — true, a multifaceted nature, and one very unlike a phenomenology, that is to say very unlike a proven, empirical, and experienced perception as defined by the common sense, or so-called common sense, of philosophers. In this sense, an eighteenth-century conception of human nature is probably much closer to Marx's than to its existentialist substitute, the human condition — a purely situational phenomenology.

Today, unfortunately, the term humanism is used to designate philosophical schools of thought, not only according to two meanings, but according to three, four, five, or six. Nowadays, everybody is a humanist. Even certain Marxists, who pride themselves on being classical rationalists, are humanists in a diluted sort of way, stripped of the liberal ideas of the previous century — embracing instead a liberalism refracted throughout the current crisis. If Marxists can claim to be humanists, then followers of the various religions — Christians, Hindus, and many others — can also claim to be humanists, as do existentialists and in general all philosophers. At present, many political movements also claim to be based on humanism. All of this converges into some sort of attempt to reinstate a philosophy that, despite its pretension, ultimately refuses to commit itself — not only from a political and social point of view, but also in a profoundly philosophical sense. When Christianity claims to be primarily humanist, it is because it refuses to commit itself, it cannot commit itself; in other words, it cannot participate in the struggle of progressive forces because, as far as this revolution is concerned, it refuses to budge from its reactionary positions. When pseudo-Marxists or liberals uphold the supremacy of the individual, it is because they are intimidated by the demands of today's world. Similarly, existentialists, as liberals, uphold the supremacy of man in general because they are incapable of formulating the commitment that these events require, and the only progressive position of which we are aware is that of Marxism. It is Marxism that poses the real problems of our era.

It is not true that man has freedom of choice in the sense that such choice allows him to endow his actions with a meaning that they would not have had without it. It is not enough to say that men can fight for freedom without knowing they are doing so; or then, if we were to attribute to such recognition its full meaning, that would mean that men can commit themselves to, and fight for, a cause that dominates them, which is to say to act within a context that is beyond them, and not only in their own terms. For in the end, if a man fights for freedom without knowing or expressly formulating for himself in what way, and for what purpose, he is fighting, that means his actions will bring about a series of consequences that would insinuate themselves into a causal web, all the facets of which he would not totally grasp, but which would nonetheless delimit his actions and give them a meaning in terms of other people's actions — not only those of other men, but of the natural environment in which such men act.

But from your point of view, "choice" is a "pre-choice" — and I keep coming back to this prefix, because I think there is always a reluctance that intervenes in this sort of pre-choice in which we are dealing with a freedom of pre-indifference. But your conception of condition and freedom is linked with a particular definition of objects that we need to discuss. Indeed, it is even from this idea of the world of objects, of instrumentality, that you derive all the rest. Just as you portray the discontinuous existences of beings, you draw a picture of a discontinuous world of objects devoid of any causality, other than this strange variety of causal relationship which is that of instrumentality: passive, incomprehensible, and contemptible. The existentialist stumbles around in a universe of instruments and filthy obstacles that he's piled one on top of another out of a bizarre need to have some of them serve others, yet marked by the stigmata — horrifying in the eyes of idealists — of "pure exteriority." This world of utensil determinism is, however, acausal. But where does such a world begin and end, when its definition is completely arbitrary and in no way consistent with modern scientific data? For us, it neither begins nor ends anywhere, because the segregation that existentialists want to subject it to in terms of nature — or rather the human condition — is unreal. In our opinion there is one world and one world only, and this world as a whole, both men and things — if you insist on this distinction — can be affected, under certain variable conditions, by the mark of objectivity. What about the instrumentality of the stars, anger, flowers? But I will not pursue that. I maintain, however, that your freedom, your idealism, is based on an arbitrary contempt for things. Yet these things are very different from your description of them. You admit that they exist in themselves, and that is already an achievement. But it is a purely privative existence, a permanent hostility. The physical and biological universe is, in your eyes, never a condition, or a source of conditioning, since this word in its fullest and practical sense has no more reality for you than does "cause." That is why the objective universe, for existentialists, is nothing but a source of disappointments, ungraspable, essentially indifferent, a perpetual "maybe" — which is to say completely the opposite of what it represents for Marxist materialism.

It is for all these reasons, and a few others, that you consider philosophical commitment to be nothing but an arbitrary decision that you refer to as freedom. You are distorting Marx's very history when you indicate that he defined a philosophy by making it political. No, commitment — or rather social and political activity — was, to the contrary, what shaped his broader ideas. His doctrines were formed by a multiplicity of experiences. It is obvious to me that Marx's philosophical thought evolved in a conscious conjunction with his political and social development. In fact, that was also more or less true for the philosophers who preceded him. If Kant was a systematic philosopher known for avoiding all political activities, that does not mean that his philosophy played no political role. (Heine, by the way, liked to call Kant the German Robespierre.) Insofar as one could admit, for example, that the development of Cartesian philosophy played no political role in Descartes's own day — which is erroneous, by the way — it has become impossible to imagine something similar in our own century. Taking a position today prior to Marxism, in any form whatsoever, is what I would call a return to radical socialism.

Inasmuch as it can inspire revolutionary ambitions, existentialism must therefore first make a commitment to a self-examination process. I doubt that it would do so willingly, but it must. Existentialism needs to weather a crisis in terms of those who defend it — a dialectical crisis, meaning that in some sense it will retain positions not devoid of value among certain of its partisans. And that seems to me all the more necessary now that I have had an opportunity to observe the

EXISTENTIALISM IS A HUMANISM

highly disturbing and clearly reactionary social inferences that some have drawn from existentialism. In concluding an analysis, one partisan wrote that phenomenology can be used very precisely today, on the social and revolutionary plane, by endowing the lower-middle class with a philosophy that would allow it to be — and become — the avant-garde of the international revolutionary movement. Through the agency of intentionality of conscience, we could endow the lower-middle class with a philosophy commensurate with its own experience — one which would enable it to become the avant-garde of the international revolutionary movement. I cite this one example, though I could well cite others. There are a number of people attached to existentialism who are very politically committed, and they can sometimes articulate political theories that, in the final analysis (and here I return to what I said in the beginning), are theories tinged with neo-liberalism or neoradical socialism. This is a clear danger. What most interests us is not to seek a dialectical consistency among all areas influenced by existentialism, but to understand the orientation of those themes that, little by little, reluctantly perhaps — on the basis of some research, theory, or attitude that you consider highly defined — may lead to something that is not quietism. Because to talk of quietism in our day is, of course, a way to give oneself the upper hand, which is certainly an impossible thing — but one that resembles a waiting game. That may not be a contradiction to certain individual commitments, but it *is* a contradiction to any commitment that seeks to takes on a collective value — especially a prescriptive one. Why shouldn't existentialism provide some guidelines? In the name of freedom? But, if it is a philosophy oriented in the direction Sartre indicated, it must provide guidelines. In 1945, it must state whether it is necessary to join the UDSR [the Democratic and Socialist Union of the Resistance, a centrist party founded in 1945], the Socialist Party, the Communist Party, or any other party; it must state whether it supports the labor party or the lower-middle-class party.

SARTRE: It is rather difficult to answer you fully, because you have said so many things. I will attempt to answer some of the points that I have jotted down. First, I think you have taken a dogmatic position. You said that we were re-adopting a pre-Marxist position, and that we were reactionary. I believe it needs to be proven that we are not trying to take a posterior position. I do not wish to argue about this, but how could you possibly have arrived at such a conception of the truth? You think there are some things that are absolutely true because you have made certain criticisms in the name of a certitude. But if all men are objects, as you say, on what is your certitude founded? You have said that it is in the name of human dignity that man refuses to treat man as an object. That is false. It is for a philosophical and logical reason: if you postulate a universe composed of objects, truth is eliminated. The world of the object is the world of the probable. You owe it to yourself to acknowledge that any theory, whether scientific or philosophic, is probable. The proof of that lies in the fact that scientific and historic theses differ and always appear in the form of hypotheses. If we acknowledge that the world of the object — the world of the probable — is unique, we will end up with nothing but a world of probabilities, and therefore, since a probability depends on a certain number of accepted truths, what is the basis of your certitude? Our subjectivism permits certitudes such that we can agree with you on the level of the probable, and justify the dogmatism that you have demonstrated during your presentation, but that does not make sense in view of the position that you are taking. If you do not define truth, how can you conceive Marx's theory other than as a doctrine that appears, disappears, and changes, and whose only value is theoretical? How can one propose a dialectic of history if one does not begin by laying down a number of rules? We find them in the Cartesian *cogito;* we can find them only by situating our discussion on a plane of subjectivity. We have never discussed the fact that men constantly treat man as an object, but, reciprocally, in order to fully understand the object as such, we need a subject that can be realized as a subject.

Next, you speak to me of a human condition that you sometimes call a "precondition" and you speak of a "predetermination." What you have missed here is that we believe in many of Marxism's views. You cannot criticize me in the same way as you would eighteenth-century people who would be totally ignorant of this issue. We have been aware for a long time of what you said about determination. For us, the real problem is to define under what conditions universality exists. Since human nature does not exist, how does one retain — in a constantly changing history — sufficient universal principles to interpret, for example, the Spartacus phenomenon, which requires one to have at least some understanding of that era? We agree on this point: human nature does not exist; in other words, every era evolves according to its own dialectical laws, and men are defined by their era, not by human nature.

NAVILLE: When you seek to interpret, you say: "It is because we are referring to a certain situation." We, on the other hand, refer to analogies or to differences between the social life of a given era and ours. If, to the contrary, we were to try to analyze this analogy in terms of an abstract type, we would not be able to do it. For example, suppose that two thousand years from now, all anyone had in order to analyze the current situation were theses on the human condition in general. What would we do to work out a retrospective analysis? We could not do it.

SARTRE: We never thought it was not necessary to analyze human conditions or individual intentions. What we call "situation" is precisely the combination of very physical and psychoanalytical conditions which, in a given era, accurately define a set.

NAVILLE: I do not believe that your definition is compatible with your texts. Nonetheless, one may conclude from them that your conception of "situation" is not—even vaguely—comparable to a Marxist conception, because it denies causation. Your definition is not precise; it vacillates conveniently back and forth from one position to another without defining them in a sufficiently exact manner. In our view, a "situation" is a constructed set revealed through a whole series of causal-type determinations, including a statistical type of causality.

SARTRE: You are talking to me about a statistical causality. That is meaningless. Can you please clearly specify what you mean by "causality"? The day when a Marxist will finally explain that to me, I will believe in Marxist causality. When we speak to you about freedom, you respond by saying: "Sorry, that has to do with causality." You are unable to explain this secret causality that makes no sense other than in Hegel's writings. You have some dream about Marxist causality.

NAVILLE: Do you admit that there is such a thing as a scientific truth? There may be fields that do not comprise even an ounce of truth. But the world of objects—you will admit this at least, I hope—is the world that science deals with. For you, though, it is a world that has only probability, and which cannot arrive at truth. Therefore the world of objects, which is that of science, cannot accept absolute truth. Yet it does arrive at a relative truth. Can you acknowledge, however, that science makes use of the notion of causality?

SARTRE: Absolutely not. Science is abstract; it also studies the variations of abstract factors, not actual causality. This concerns universal factors on a level in which relationships can always be studied. Marxism, on the other hand, has to do with the study of a unique set in which we seek a causality. It is not at all the same thing as scientific causality.

NAVILLE: You used the example of a young man who came to see you, which you elaborated at length.

SARTRE: Wasn't that in connection with freedom?

NAVILLE: You had to answer him. I would have inquired about his capabilities, his age, and his financial resources. I would have examined his relationship with his mother. It's possible I might have offered an opinion, but I most certainly would have tried to settle on a precise point of view, which might have proven false when put into action, but I certainly would have encouraged him to do something.

SARTRE: If he comes to you asking for advice, he has already chosen a course of action. In practical terms, I could very well have given him advice. But since his goal was freedom, I wanted him to be free to decide. In any case, I knew what he was going to do, and that is what he did.

A Commentary on *The Stranger*

Camus's *The Stranger* had scarcely been in print before it attracted a great deal of attention.[1] People kept saying that it was "the best book since the end of the war." Among the literary productions of its time, the novel was itself a stranger. It came to us from the other side of the horizon, the other side of the sea; in that bitter spring without coal, it spoke to us of the sun, not as some exotic wonder but in a tone of weary familiarity used by people who have indulged in it too much. It did not set out to rebury the old regime on its own say-so, or to fill us with feelings of our own unworthiness. While reading this book, we recalled that there had once been works that did not attempt to prove anything, content just to stand on their own merits. But this novel's gratuitousness was also accompanied by a certain ambiguity. What were we to make of this character who, on the day after his mother's death, "went swimming, began a pointless affair, went to the movies to see a comedy," killed an Arab "because of the sun," claimed, on the eve of his execution, that he "had been happy and still was," and hoped there would be lots of spectators around the scaffold "to welcome him with cries of hatred"? "He's a nut, a poor fool," some people said, while others, more insightful, said "he's an innocent." The significance of this innocence was not yet understood.

In *The Myth of Sisyphus*, which appeared a few months later, Camus provided us with a precise commentary on his work: his hero was neither good nor bad, neither moral nor immoral. Such categories do not apply to him. He belongs to a very particular species for which the author reserves the name "absurd." But in Camus's work, this word takes on two very different meanings. The "absurd" is both a factual state and the lucid awareness that some people acquire from that state. The "absurd" man is one who does not hesitate to draw inevitable conclusions from a fundamental absurdity. In this we find the same displacement of meaning as when we give the name "swing" to the young generation that dances to "swing" music. What, then, does "absurd" mean as a factual state or as a set of givens? Nothing less than man's relationship to the world. Primary absurdity manifests itself as a schism — the schism between man's aspirations for unity and the insurmountable dualism of mind and nature, between man's drive to attain the eternal and the *finite* nature of his existence, between the "concern" that constitutes his very essence and the vanity of his efforts. Death, the irreducible pluralism of truths and of beings, the unintelligibility of reality, chance — these are the core components of the absurd.

These themes are not really very new, and Camus does not present them as such. They had been explored as early as the seventeenth century through a dry, plain, and contemplative rationalism, which is typically French, and in which they found expression as platitudes of classical pessimism. Was it not Pascal who stressed that "the natural misfortune of our mortal and feeble condition is so wretched that when we consider it closely, nothing can console us"? Was it not he who put reason in its place? Would he not have enthusiastically approved of this comment by Camus: "The world is neither (totally) rational, nor so irrational"? Does he not show us that "custom" and "diversion" conceal from man his "nothingness, his forlornness, his inadequacy, his impotence, and his emptiness"? By dint of the impersonal style used in *The Myth of Sisyphus* and the themes explored in his essays, Camus must be placed in the great tradition of those French moralists whom Charles Andler has rightly called "Nietzsche's precursors." As for the doubts that he has raised about the scope of our reasoning powers, they are in line with the most recent tradition of French epistemology. If we consider scientific nominalism — Poincaré, Duhem, and Meyerson — it is easier for us to understand the reproach made by our author against modern science: "You tell me of an invisible planetary system in which electrons revolve around a nucleus. You explain the world to me by means of an image. I realize then that you have arrived at a poetic understanding of things."[2] This idea was also expressed, almost at the same time, by another writer who was drawing from the same material when he wrote: "Physics uses mechanical, dynamic, or even psychological models indifferently, as if, liberated from ontological pretensions, it were indifferent to the classical antinomies of mechanism or dynamism which imply a nature-in-itself."[3] Camus seems to pride himself on quoting Jaspers, Heidegger, and Kierkegaard, whom he seems not to have always truly understood. But his real masters are to be found elsewhere: the way in which he reasons, the clarity of his ideas, the cut of his essayistic style, and a certain kind of solar, orderly, ceremonious, and desolate melancholy, all reveal a classical temperament, a Mediterranean. His very method ("only through a balance of evidence and lyricism can we simultaneously achieve emotion and lucidity") brings to mind the old "passionate geometries" of Pascal and Rousseau and relate him, for example, far more to Charles Maurras — that other Mediterranean from whom he nonetheless differs in so many respects — than to a German phenomenologist or a Danish existentialist.[4]

But Camus would no doubt be willing to agree with all this. As he sees it, his originality lies in stretching his ideas to the limit; indeed, his aim is not to produce a collection of pessimistic maxims. The absurd, to be sure, resides neither in man nor in the world, if one considers each separately. But since man's essential nature is "being-in-the-world," the absurd is ultimately an inseparable part of the human condition. Thus, the absurd is not at all primarily the object of a simple notion; it is revealed to us in a bleak light. "Get up, take subway, work four hours at the office or plant, eat, take subway, work four hours, eat, sleep — Monday-Tuesday-Wednesday-Thursday-Friday-Saturday — always the same routine . . . ," and then, suddenly, "the stage set collapses," and we are immersed in hopeless lucidity. So if we manage to reject the misleading promises of religion or existential philosophies, we come into possession of certain basic truths: the world is chaos, a "divine equivalence born of anarchy"; and tomorrow does not exist, since we all die. "In a universe suddenly deprived of illusions and enlightenment, man feels like a stranger. This exile is irrevocable, since he has no memories of a lost homeland, nor any hope of a promised land." That is because man *is not* the world. "If I were a tree among other trees . . . this life would have a meaning, or rather this problem would have none, for I would be part of this world. I *would be* this world in opposition to which I now find myself, as a fully conscious being. . . . It is this preposterous reason that sets me against all of creation." The latter partially explains the title of Camus's novel: the "stranger" is man confronting the world. Camus could just as well have chosen for the title of his novel the name of a work by George Gissing: *Born in Exile*. The stranger is also a man among men. "There are days when . . . you find that the person you've loved has become a stranger." The stranger is, finally, myself in relation to myself — that is, natural man in relation to mind: "The stranger who, at certain moments, confronts us in a mirror."[5]

But it is more than that: there is a passion of the absurd. The absurd man will not commit suicide; he wants to live, without relinquishing any of his certainty, without a future, without hope, without illusion and without resignation, either. The absurd man asserts himself by revolting. He stares at death with passionate attention and this fascination liberates him. He experiences the "divine irresponsibility" of a man sentenced to die. Since God does not exist and we all must die, everything is permissible. One experience is as good as another, so what matters is simply to acquire as many of them as possible. "For the absurd man, the ideal is the present and the succession of present moments before an ever-conscious spirit."[6] Confronted with this "quantitative ethic," all values collapse. Projected into this world, the absurd man, rebellious and irresponsible, has "nothing to prove." He is *innocent*, as innocent as Somerset Maugham's primitive tribesmen before the clergyman comes to teach them Good and Evil, what is permitted and what is forbidden. For this man, *everything* is permissible. He is as innocent as Prince Mishkin, who "lives in a perpetual present, tinged with smiles and indifference." Innocent in every sense of the word, an "idiot," too, if you like. And now we fully understand the title of Camus's novel. The stranger he wants to portray is precisely one of those terrible "idiots" who shock a society by not accepting the rules of its game. He lives among strangers, but he is a stranger to them, too. That is why some people grow fond of him — like Marie, his mistress, who likes him "because he's odd." Others, like the courtroom crowd whose hatred he feels suddenly rising against him, hate him for the same reason. And we ourselves, opening the book, and being not yet familiar with the feeling of the absurd, will try in vain to judge him according to our customary standards: for us, too, he is a stranger.

Thus the shock you felt when you first opened the book and read, "It occurred to me that anyway one more Sunday was over, that Mama was buried now, that I would go back to work and that, really, nothing had changed," was intentional.[7] It was the result of your first encounter with the absurd. But you were probably hoping, as you continued reading the book, that your uneasiness would fade, everything would gradually become clear, be made reasonable, and explained. Your hopes were dashed: *The Stranger* is not a book that explains anything. The absurd man does not explain, he describes. Nor is it a book that proves anything. Camus merely presents something and is not concerned about justifying what is fundamentally unjustifiable. *The Myth of Sisyphus* will later teach us to interpret our author's novel. It is in the latter that we discover the theory of the absurd novel. Although the absurdity of the human condition is its sole theme, it is not a novel with a political or social message. It is not the product of a "smug" kind of thinking, intent on supplying formal proofs, but, to the contrary, the product of a "limited, mortal and rebellious" thought. The novel's very existence is proof of the futility of rational reasoning. "The choice that [great novelists] have made to rely on images rather than on arguments reveals a certain kind of idea that they all shared — a conviction of the futility of all explanatory principles, and of the communicative power of words that appeal to the senses."[8]

Thus, the very fact that Camus delivers his message in the form of a novel reveals a proud humility. This is not resignation, but an outraged acknowledgement of the limitations of human thought. It is true that he felt obliged to make a philosophical translation of his fictional message. *The Myth of Sisyphus* is precisely that, and we shall see later how we are to interpret the relationship of these two works. But, in any event, the presence of the translation does not alter the gratuitousness of the novel. The writer of the absurd has, indeed, lost even the illusion that his work is necessary. On the contrary, he wants us to be constantly aware of its contingent nature. As its epigraph, he would have us write, "Might not have been," just as Gide wished his readers would envision at the end of *The Counterfeiters:* "May be continued." This novel might not have been, any more than this or that stone, stream, or face. It is a present that simply offers itself, like all other presents in this world. It does not even have this subjective necessity that artists readily claim for their works when they say, "I had to write it, I had to get it off my chest." In this book, we reencounter one of the themes of surrealist terrorism, filtered through the light of a classic sun. A work of art is only a page torn from a life. It expresses this life, of course, but it could have very well not expressed it. No matter, for everything has the same value, whether it be writing *The Possessed* or drinking a cup of coffee. Camus does not demand of the reader that attentive solicitude that writers do who "have sacrificed their lives to art." *The Stranger* is just a sheet torn from his life. And since the most absurd life must be that which is most sterile, his novel aims at being magnificently sterile. Art is a futile act of generosity. We need not be too concerned about that, for hidden beneath Camus's paradoxes, I find some of Kant's very wise observations on the "endless end" of the beautiful. Such, in any event, is *The Stranger*, a work detached from a life, unjustified and unjustifiable, sterile, fleeting, already forsaken by its author, abandoned for other presents. And that is how we must accept it — as an abrupt communion between two individuals, the author and the reader — beyond reason — in the realm of the absurd.

This gives us some indication of how we are to regard the hero of *The Stranger*. If Camus had wanted to write a novel with a political or social message, it would have been easy for him to portray a civil servant lording it over his family, who is suddenly struck with the intuition of the absurd, which he resists for a while before finally resolving to live out the fundamental absurdity of his condition. The reader would have been convinced right with the character, and for the same reasons. Or, he could have related the life of one of those saints of the absurd so dear to his heart and whom he describes in *The Myth of Sisyphus:* Don Juan, the Actor, the Conqueror, the Creator. But he did not do so, and Meursault, the hero of *The Stranger,* remains ambiguous even to readers who are familiar with the theories of the absurd. Naturally, we are assured that he is absurd, and that his dominant character trait is a pitiless lucidity. Besides, in more ways than one he was created to provide a concerted illustration of the theories presented in *The Myth of Sisyphus.* In the latter work, for example, Camus writes: "A man is more of a man because of what he does not say than what he does say." Meursault personifies this virile silence, this refusal to over-indulge in words: "[He was asked] if he had noticed that I was withdrawn, and all he admitted to was that I did not waste words." Two lines before this, the same witness has just testified that Meursault "was a man." "[He was asked] what he meant by that, and he said that everyone knew what he meant."[9]

Similarly, in *The Myth of Sisyphus,* Camus expounds on the subject of love. He writes, "We call love that which binds us to certain human beings based solely on a collective way of seeing for which books and legends are responsible." And in the same vein, we read in *The Stranger:* "So she wanted to know whether I loved her. I answered . . . that it didn't mean anything, but that I probably didn't love her." From this vantage point, the debate that flares in the courtroom and in the reader's mind, "Did Meursault love his mother?" is doubly absurd. First of all, as the lawyer asks, "Is he accused of having buried his mother or of having killed a man?" But the words "to love" are the most meaningless of all. Meursault probably put his mother into a nursing home because he was short of money and because "they had nothing more to say to each other." And he probably did not go to see her often "because it wasted [his] Sunday—not to mention the effort involved in going to the bus station, buying tickets, and taking a two-hour trip."[10] But what does this mean? Isn't he living entirely in the present, fully indulging his passing moods? What we call a feeling is merely the abstract unity and the meaning of discontinuous impressions. I am not constantly thinking about the people I love, yet I claim to love them even when I am not thinking about them—and I would be capable of compromising my well-being in the name of an abstract feeling, in the absence of any real and immediate emotion. Meursault thinks and acts in a different way: he has no desire to know these noble, continuous, and identical feelings. For him, neither love nor even romantic relationships exist. All that counts is the present—the concrete. He goes to see his mother when he feels like it, and that's that. If the desire is there, it will be strong enough to compel him to get on the bus, just as another concrete desire will be strong enough to make this sluggard run at full speed and catch a ride on the back of a moving truck. Yet he still calls his mother by the tender, childish name of "Mama," and he never misses a chance to understand her and identify with her. "All I know of love is that mixture of desire, tenderness, and intelligence that binds me to a particular being."[11]

We thus see that we should not fail to consider the *theoretical* side of Meursault's character. Similarly, the main purpose of his many adventures is to highlight some aspect or other of the basic absurdity of things. *The Myth of Sisyphus*, for example, extols the "sense of perfect freedom experienced by the condemned prisoner for whom, at dawn on an appointed day, the prison doors swing open."[12] In order to make us taste this dawn, this freedom, Camus sentences his hero to capital punishment. "How could I have failed to see," says Meursault, "that nothing was more important than an execution . . . and that, in a way, it was even the only really worthwhile thing for a man!" We could cite many such examples and quotations. However, this lucid, indifferent, taciturn man was not merely produced to serve a cause. Once the character had been roughly outlined, Meursault probably completed Camus's task himself, already possessed of a substance of his own. Still, his absurdity seems to have been attributed rather than acquired — that is the way he is, and that's that. He does finally get his moment of revelation on the last page, but he has always lived according to Camus's standards. If there were a grace in the realm of the absurd, we would have to say that he has received it. He does not seem to ask himself any of the questions explored in *The Myth of Sisyphus*. Meursault does not seem to be indignant about his death sentence.

He was happy, he did as he liked, and his happiness does not seem to have been affected by any inner gnawing so frequently mentioned by Camus in his essay, which stems from the blinding presence of death. His very indifference often seems like indolence, for instance on that Sunday when he stays home out of pure laziness, and admits to having been "a little bored." The character thus remains singularly impenetrable, even from a vantage point of the absurd. He is no Don Juan, no Don Quixote of the absurd; in fact, he often seems more like Sancho Panza. He is there before us, he exists, and we can neither understand nor quite judge him. In a word, he is alive, but his fictional density is the only thing that can make him acceptable to us.

However, it would be a mistake to view *The Stranger* as a completely gratuitous work. As we have said, Camus distinguishes between the *feeling* and the *notion* of the absurd. In this respect, he writes, "Like great works, deep feelings always convey more meaning than they are aware that they do. . . . Intense feelings carry with them their own universe — splendid or wretched, as the case may be."[13] A bit further on he adds, "The feeling of the absurd is not the same as the *idea* of the absurd. The idea is grounded in the feeling, that is all. It does not fully express . . . it." We could say that the aim of *The Myth of Sisyphus* is to convey the *idea* of the absurd, and that of *The Stranger* to convey the *feeling*. The order in which the two works were published seems to confirm this theory. *The Stranger*, the first to appear, plunges us without comment into the "climate" of the absurd; the essay then arrives to shed light on the landscape. Now, "absurdity" means divorce, discrepancy. Thus *The Stranger* was meant to be a novel of discrepancy, divorce, and disorientation. Hence its clever structure: on the one hand there is the amorphous, everyday flow of reality as it is experienced, and, on the other, the edifying reconstruction of this reality by human reasoning and speech. When first brought face-to-face with simple reality, the reader confronts it without being able to recognize it in its rational transposition. This is the source of the feeling of the absurd — that is, of our inability to *conceive*, using our concepts and our words, what occurs in the world. Meursault buries his mother, takes a mistress, and commits a crime. These various facts will be related by witnesses at his trial, and arranged and explained by the public prosecutor. Meursault will have the impression that people are talking about someone else. Everything is orchestrated to lead up to the moment of Marie's sudden outburst. After giving her account on the witness stand (a story composed according to human rules), she bursts into tears and tells the prosecutor "that wasn't it, there was something else, he was forcing her to say the opposite of what she really thought." This hall of mirrors has been used frequently since *The Counterfeiters*, and does not constitute Camus's originality. But the problem to be solved requires him to use an original form; if we are to feel the discrepancy between the prosecutor's conclusions and the actual circumstances of the murder, and if, on finishing the book, we are to retain the impression of an absurd justice that can never comprehend or even confront the deeds it intends to punish, we must first have been placed in contact with reality, or with one of these circumstances. But in order to establish this contact, Camus, like the prosecutor, has only words and concepts at his disposal. In assembling his thoughts, he must use words to describe a world that precedes words.

The first part of *The Stranger* could have been given the same title as that of a recent book — *Translated from Silence*. Here we touch on a disease common to many contemporary writers, the first signs of which I find in the works of Jules Renard. I shall call it "the obsession with silence." Paulhan would certainly regard it as an effect of literary terrorism. It has taken a thousand forms, ranging from the surrealists' automatic writing to Jean-Jacques Bernard's celebrated "theater of silence." That is because silence, in the words of Heidegger, is *the* authentic mode of speech. Only he who can talk keeps silent. Camus talks a great deal — in *The Myth of Sisyphus* he is downright chatty. Yet he reveals his love of silence. He quotes Kierkegaard: "The surest way of being mute is not to hold your tongue, but to talk," and Camus himself adds that "a man is more of a man because of what he does not say than what he does say."[14] Thus, in *The Stranger*, he has attempted *to be silent*. But how can one be silent with words? How can one convey the unthinkable and disorderly succession of presents through concepts? This challenge involves resorting to a new technique.

What is this new technique? I have been told: "It's Kafka written by Hemingway." I confess that I have found no trace of Kafka in it. Camus's views are wholly of this world. Kafka is the novelist of impossible transcendence; for him, the universe is full of signs that we cannot understand; there is something behind the scenery. For Camus, to the contrary, the tragedy of human existence lies in the absence of any transcendence. "I do not know whether this world has a meaning that eludes me. But I do know that I do not know this meaning and that, for the time being, it is impossible for me to know it. What can a meaning beyond my condition mean to me? I can comprehend only in human terms. I understand what I touch, what offers resistance." He is not concerned, then, with arranging words so as to suggest an inhuman, indecipherable order; the inhuman is merely the disorderly, the mechanical. There is nothing dubious in his work, nothing disquieting, nothing implied. *The Stranger* gives us a succession of luminously clear views. If they bewilder us, it is only because of their number and the absence of any common link between them. Camus's favorite hours of the day are clear mornings and evenings, and relentless afternoons. His favorite season is Algiers' eternal summer. In his universe, there is scarcely any place for night. When he does speak of it, it is in these terms: "I woke up with stars in my face. Country sounds reached my ears. Aromas of night, earth, and salt soothed my temples. The wonderful peace of that sleepy summer invaded me like a tide."[15] The man who wrote these lines is as far removed as possible from the anxieties of a Kafka. He is very much at peace within disorder. The obstinate blindness of nature may irritate, but also comforts, him. Its irrationality is merely a negative thing. The absurd man is a humanist; he knows only the good things of this world.

The comparison with Hemingway seems more fruitful. There is an evident relationship between the two styles. Equally short sentences can be found in both texts. Each sentence refuses to exploit the momentum gained from the preceding one. Each is a new beginning. Each is like a snapshot of a gesture or an object. With each new gesture and new object comes a new sentence. Nonetheless, I am not fully convinced: the existence of an "American" narrative technique has unquestionably helped Camus. But, strictly speaking, I doubt whether it has influenced him. Even in *Death in the Afternoon*, which is not a novel, Hemingway retains that halting style of narration that shoots each separate sentence out of the void with a sort of respiratory spasm: he and his style are interchangeable. We already know that Camus has a different style, a ceremonious one. Yet even in *The Stranger*, he occasionally raises the tone of his voice; his sentences then take on a larger and more flowing movement. "The cry of the paper boys in the already leisurely air, the last birds in the square, the calls of the sandwich vendors, the howl of trolleys on the high curves of the city, and that distant murmur in the sky just as night begins to spill over the port—all of these seemed to be forming a blind man's path that I had known long before entering prison."[16] Beneath the transparency of Meursault's breathless account, I catch a glimpse of a broader underlying poetic prose that is probably Camus's personal mode of expression. If *The Stranger* exhibits such visible traces of the American technique, it was intentional. Of all the tools at his disposal, Camus chose the one that he felt would serve his purpose best. I doubt whether he will use it again in his future works.

Let us examine the plot a little more closely so that we can get a clearer idea of his methods. "Men also secrete the inhuman," writes Camus. "Sometimes, in moments of lucidity, the mechanical aspect of their gestures and their senseless pantomime make everything around them seem stupid." This quality should be rendered first: from its opening pages *The Stranger* puts us "in a state of uneasiness as we confront man's inhumanity." But what are the particular instances that may provoke such uneasiness in us? *The Myth of Sisyphus* gives us an example of this. "A man is talking on the telephone behind a glass partition. We cannot hear him, but we can see his senseless mimicry. We wonder why he is alive."[17] We immediately know the answer—almost too well, for the example reveals a certain bias in the author. The gesturing of a man on the telephone—whom you cannot hear—is really only *rela-*

tively absurd, because it is part of an incomplete circuit. But if you open the booth door and then put your ear to the receiver, the circuit is complete and the human activity makes sense again. In honesty, therefore, one would have to say that there are only relative absurdities that exist solely in relation to "absolute rationalities." However, we are dealing with a matter not of honesty, but of art. Camus has a method in mind: he is going to insert a glass partition between the reader and his characters. Does anything look more foolish than men behind a glass window? Glass seems to let everything through. It blocks only one thing: the meaning of their gestures. The glass still needs to be chosen: it will be the Stranger's consciousness, which is really transparent, since we see everything it sees. However, it is designed in such a way that things are transparent and meanings opaque.

"From then on, everything happened very quickly. The men went up to the coffin with a sheet. The priest, his attendants, the director, and I went outside. In front of the door was a lady whom I didn't know. 'Monsieur Meursault,' said the director. I didn't catch the lady's name, and gathered only that she was a nurse who had been ordered to be present. Without smiling, she nodded her long, bony face. Then we stood aside to make room for the body to pass."[18]

Some men are dancing behind a glass partition. A consciousness has been interposed between them and the reader — something insignificant, a translucent curtain, a pure passivity that records all the facts. And there you have it: precisely because it is passive, this consciousness records only the facts. The reader is unaware of this insertion. But what is the assumption implied by this kind of narrative technique? In short, what had once been melodic structure has been transformed into a sum of invariant elements. Supposedly this succession of *movements* is rigorously identical with the *act* considered as a whole. Are we not dealing here with the analytic assumption that any reality is reducible to a sum of elements? Although analysis may be the instrument of science, it is also the instrument of humor. If, in wishing to describe a rugby match, I write: "I saw adults in shorts fighting and throwing themselves on the ground in order to send a leather ball between a pair of wooden posts," I have summed up what I *saw*, but I have deliberately omitted giving the facts any meaning — I was being humorous. Camus's story is analytical and humorous. Like all artists, he *lies*, because he pretends to reproduce raw experience, and because he slyly filters out all of the meaningful links that are also part of the experience. That is what Hume did when he stated that he could find nothing in experience but isolated impressions. That is what today's American neorealists are still doing when they deny the existence of anything other than external relations between phenomena. By contrast, contemporary philosophy has established that meanings are also part of immediate data. But exploring this would take us too far afield. Let us simply indicate that the absurd man's universe is the neorealists' analytical world. This method has proved its worth in literature: it was used in Voltaire's *Ingenue* and *Micromégas*, as well as in Swift's *Gulliver's Travels*. For the eighteenth century had its own strangers — in the form of "noble savages" — who, when transported to an unknown civilization, would perceive facts before they could grasp their meaning. Was not the effect of this discrepancy precisely to arouse in the reader the feeling of the absurd? Camus seems to have recalled this on several occasions, particularly when he shows us his hero reflecting on the reasons for his imprisonment.[19]

However, it is this analytical process that explains the use of the American technique in *The Stranger*. The presence of death at the end of our road has made our future go up in smoke. Our life has "no tomorrow" — it is merely a series of instants. What can this mean, if not that the absurd man is applying his analytical mind to time? Where Bergson saw a structure that could not be broken down, Camus perceives only a series of instants. It is the plurality of incommunicable moments that will finally account for the plurality of beings. What our author borrows from Hemingway is thus the discontinuity between clipped sentences that imitate the discontinuity of time. We are now better prepared to understand the "slice-of-life" style of his narrative. Each sentence is a present instant, but not an indecisive one, that stands out, and remains with us long enough to affect the following one. Each sentence is clear, flawless, and self-contained. It is separated by a void from the following one, just as Descartes's instant is distinct from one following it. The world is destroyed and reborn from one sentence to the next. When speech makes its appearance, it is a creation *ex nihilo*. The sentences in *The Stranger* are islands. We tumble from sentence to sentence, from nothingness to nothingness.

In order to emphasize the isolation of each sentence unit, Camus has chosen to tell his story in the present perfect tense. The simple past is the tense of continuity: "Il se promena longtemps" [He walked a long time]. These words refer us to a pluperfect—to a future. The reality of the sentence is the verb, the act, with its transitive character and its transcendence. "Il s'est promené longtemps" [He has walked a long time] dissimulates the verbality of the verb: the verb is broken, split in two. On one hand, we find a past participle that has lost all transcendence and is as inert as an object; on the other, we find the verb "être," which possesses only a copulative sense, and joins the participle to the substantive, like the attribute to the subject. The transitive nature of the verb has vanished and the sentence has frozen: its reality is now the noun. Instead of acting as a bridge between past and future, it is merely a small, isolated, self-sufficient substance. If, in addition to all the rest, we were careful to reduce the sentence as much as possible to the main proposition, its internal structure would achieve perfect simplicity and thereby gain cohesiveness. It becomes truly indivisible—an atom of time.

The sentences are not, of course, arranged in relation to each other; they are simply juxtaposed. All causal links are carefully avoided, since they would introduce in the narrative the kernel of an explanation and, between instants, an order other than that of pure succession. Consider this passage: "She asked me, a moment later, if I loved her. *I answered that it didn't mean anything, but that I probably didn't love her. She looked sad.* But while preparing lunch, for no reason at all she suddenly laughed in such a way that I kissed her. Just then, the noise of an argument broke out at Raymond's place."[20] We have cited two sentences that conceal, as unobtrusively as possible, a causal link under the mere appearance of succession. When it is absolutely necessary to allude to a preceding sentence, the author uses words like "and," "but," "then," and "just then," which evoke nothing but disjunction, opposition, or mere addition. The relations between these temporal units are external, like those that the neorealists established between objects. Reality appears on the scene with no introduction and disappears without being destroyed. The world dissolves and is reborn with each pulsation of time. But we must not think it generates itself, for it is inert. Any activity on its part would tend to substitute formidable forces for the reassuring disorder created by chance. A nineteenth-century naturalist would have written, "A bridge spanned the river." Camus will have none of this anthropomorphism. He will say, "Over the river there was a bridge." That way, we immediately sense the object's passivity. *It is there:* plain and undifferentiated. "There were four men in black in the room. . . . In front of the door was a lady I didn't know. . . . In front of the door, the hearse was waiting.... Standing next to the hearse was the director. . . ."[21] People used to say that Jules Renard would end by writing: "The hen is laying an egg." Camus and many other contemporary writers would write: "There is the hen and she is laying an egg." That is because they like things for their own sake, and do not want to dilute them in the flux of duration. "There is water": in this we hold a small piece of eternity — passive, impenetrable, incommunicable, and gleaming. What a sensual delight — if we could only touch it! To the absurd man, this is the only good thing in this world. That is why the novelist prefers this transient twinkling of tiny sparkles, each bringing us a moment of pleasure, to an organized narrative. This is what leads Camus to think that in writing *The Stranger* he remains silent. His sentence does not belong to the universe of discourse. It has neither ramifications nor extensions, nor internal structure. Like Valéry's Sylph, it might be defined as:

> *On the sly:*
> *A bare breast glimpsed*
> *Between an open shirt.*

Its exact measure corresponds to the duration of a silent intuition.

In such terms, can we speak of the body of Camus's novel as constituting something whole? All the sentences in his book equate to the same thing, as do all of the absurd man's experiences. Each one stands on its own and projects the others into the void. Yet, as a result, no single one of them stands out, except for the rare moments in which the author, abandoning his own principles, indulges in poetry. Even dialogs are integrated into the narrative. Dialog is the moment of explanation, of meaning, and to privilege it in any way would be to acknowledge that meanings exist. Instead, Camus shortens dialog, compresses it, and often expresses it in the form of indirect discourse, stripping it of all typographic prominence in such a way that spoken phrases appear to have no more significance than narrative descriptions. They flash for an instant and then disappear, like lightning, or like a sound or an odor. Thus, when you start reading the book, you feel as if you were listening to a monotonous, nasal Arab chant, rather than reading a novel. You may expect the novel to be like one of those melodies Courteline describes, which "disappear and never return," and which come to a sudden stop, for some unknown reason. But the work gradually takes shape on its own, before the reader's eyes, revealing its solid substructure. There is not a single unnecessary detail — not one that is not brought up again later on and used in the trial proceedings. And when we close the book, we realize that it could not have had any other beginning, or any other ending. In this world that has been carefully stripped of its causality and presented as absurd, the slightest incident counts. There is not a single one of them that does not help to lead the hero to crime and capital punishment. *The Stranger* is a classical work, a clearly orchestrated work, composed about, and against, the absurd.

Was this really what the author set out to do? I do not know; I am simply presenting my opinion as a reader.

How are we to categorize this clear-cut work, so carefully composed beneath its apparent disorder, so "human," so obvious, too, once you have the key? It cannot be called a story, for a story explains and coordinates as it narrates. It substitutes causal order for chronological sequence. Camus calls it a novel. Yet a novel requires continuous duration, development, and the manifest presence of irreversible time. It is not without hesitation that I would use the term "novel" for this succession of inert presents that allows us to see, from underneath, the mechanical economy of a deliberately staged piece of writing. Or, if it is a novel, then it is a novel in the manner of *Zadig* and *Candide*, a short moralistic novel — one with ironic portraits and a hint of satire — a novel that, despite the influence of German existentialists and American novelists, ultimately remains reminiscent of a tale by Voltaire.[22]

Notes

PREFACE TO THE 1996 FRENCH EDITION

1. There were, however, already some young philosophers—in a circle whose members were starting to outnumber his former students —who were paying close attention to what Sartre wrote, such as Francis Jeanson, who published *Le Problème moral et la pensée de Sartre* (Paris: Éditions du Myrte, 1947).

2. Pierre Emmanuel, "Qu'est-ce que l'existentialisme? Bilan d'une offensive," *Les Lettres françaises*, November 24, 1945. Emmanuel furthermore said that existentialism was a "mental disease" ("Réflexions sur une mise au point," in the review *Fontaine*, April 1945).

3. It was not his first attempt: he had proposed a definition of existentialism and replied to the Communist criticisms in the weekly *Action*. "À propos de l'existentialisme: Mise au point," *Action*, December 29, 1944; reprinted in *Les Écrits de Sartre*, ed. Michel Contat and Michel Rybalka (Paris: Gallimard, 1970).

4. Introduction to *Les Temps modernes*, in the first issue of the review, October 1945, reprinted in *Situations*, vol. 2 (Paris: Gallimard, 1948).

5. M.-A. Burnier, *Les Existentialistes et la politique* (Paris: Gallimard, 1966).

6. *Les Temps modernes*, nos. 9 and 10, June and July 1946, reprinted in *Situations*, vol. 3 (Paris: Gallimard, 1949).

7. His theory of original freedom, from which were derived the notions of commitment and responsibility, merely offers a glimpse of what was to become an ethic he vowed to devote a future work to (see *Being and Nothingness*, part 4, and conclusion).

8. Pierre Naville (1904–1993), a journalist and sociologist, as well as a former surrealist and Communist militant, was expelled from the Communist Party in 1928 for Trotskyism. He was the leader of the Trotskyist movement from 1929 to 1939. In 1945, he founded *La Revue internationale* and established closer ties with the party. When recalling this era, his friend Maurice Nadeau attested: "For the survivors that we are in more than one sense, including being survivors of 'Trotskyism,' we must rethink the situation with the help of the only compass we have left: Marxism." Maurice Nadeau, *Grâces leur soient rendues* [May We Give Thanks to Them] (Paris: Albin Michel, 1990).

9. *La Revue internationale*, no. 4, April 1946 (emphasis added). Of his fruitless attempts to communicate with the Marxists, Sartre said, "The fact is that contemporary Marxists are incapable of putting aside their own opinions: they *reject* their adversaries' slogans (out of fear, hatred, or laziness) at the very time when they want to open up their ranks to them. This contradiction blocks them." Jean-Paul Sartre, "Search for a Method," in *Critique of Dialectical Reason*, vol. 1, revised edition (Paris: Gallimard, 1985).

10. Jean-Paul Sartre, *Vérité et existence* [Truth and Existence], published posthumously (Paris: Gallimard, 1989).

11. Sartre, "Search for a Method."

INTRODUCTION

1. Jean-Paul Sartre, *Situations*, vol. 3 (Paris: Gallimard, 1949), 11.

2. Albert Camus, *Alger republication*, October 20, 1938, and March 12, 1939.

3. By Pierre Bourdieu, for example.

4. *The Myth of Sisyphus* was published a few months after *The Stranger*. In 1943, Sartre published *Being and Nothingness*, a 724-page philosophical

tome representing the "core" of his intellectual enterprise, at least up until the 1960s, and from which his novels, plays, and critical writings, et cetera, spring like so many illustrations of his thought.

5. Sartre, who had lost his father at a young age, related to the question of origins in his own idiosyncratic way. In *The Words*, for example, he describes his own neuroses with amazing virtuosity: "I was born from writing: before, there was nothing but a succession of mirrors."

6. *Cahiers du sud*, 1945, reprinted in *Situations*, vol. 1 (Paris: Gallimard, 1947); "Forgers of Myths: The Young Playwrights of France," *Theater Arts*, June 1946, 324–335; "New Writing in France: The Resistance 'taught that literature is no fancy activity independent of politics,'" *Vogue*, July 1945, 84–85.

EXISTENTIALISM IS A HUMANISM

1. Heidegger refused to call himself an atheistic existentialist in his *Lettre sur l'humanisme* (1946).

2. "Notes premières de l'homme," *Les Temps modernes*, no. 1, October 1945.

3. The announced subject of the lecture was "Is Existentialism a Humanism?"

4. "À propos de l'existentialisme: Mise au point," *Action*, December 29, 1944; reprinted in *Les Écrits de Sartre*, ed. Michel Contat and Michel Rybalka (Paris: Gallimard, 1970).

A COMMENTARY ON *THE STRANGER*

1. Albert Camus, *L'Étranger* [The Stranger] (Paris: Gallimard, 1942). Sartre's essay on *The Stranger* was originally published in *Cahiers du sud* (February 1943), and reprinted in *Situations*, vol. 1 (Paris: Gallimard, 1947).

2. Albert Camus, *The Myth of Sisyphus* (Paris: Gallimard, 1942), 35.

3. Maurice Merleau-Ponty, *La Structure du comportement* (Paris: La Renaissance du Livre, 1942), 1.

4. Camus, *Myth of Sisyphus*, 16.

5. Ibid., 27, 18, 74, 29.

6. Ibid., 88.

7. Camus, *The Stranger*, 36.

8. Camus, *Myth of Sisyphus*, 138.

9. Camus, *The Stranger*, 121.

10. Camus, *Myth of Sisyphus*, 102; Camus, *The Stranger*, 59, 12.

11. Camus, *Myth of Sisyphus*, 102.

12. Ibid., 83.

13. Ibid., 25.

14. Ibid., 42. Also consult Brice Parain's theory of language and his conception of silence.

15. Camus, *The Stranger*, 158.

16. Ibid., 128. See also pp. 81–82, 158–159, etc.

17. Camus, *Myth of Sisyphus*, 29.

18. Camus, *The Stranger*, 23.

19. Ibid., 103, 104.

20. Ibid., 51.

21. Ibid., 23.

22. The ironic portraits in *The Stranger* are those of the pimp, the judge, and the prosecuting attorney.

About the Author

*B*orn in Paris on June 21, 1905, Jean-Paul Sartre — like his classmates from the École Normale Supérieure — was very young when he first began to find fault with the values and traditions of his social class, the bourgeoisie. He taught for a while at Lycée du Havre, then pursued his academic training in philosophy at the French Institute in Berlin. The originality of his thought, already evident in his earliest philosophic works, *L'Imagination* (1936) [published in English as Imagination: A Psychological Critique (1962)], *Esquisse d'une théorie des émotions* (1939) [Sketch for a Theory of the Emotions (1962)], and *L'Imaginaire* (1940) [The Psychology of Imagination (1948)], would ultimately lead him to existentialism, whose arguments are expanded on in *L'Être et le néant* (1943) [Being and Nothingness (1956)], and in *L'Existentialisme est un humanisme* (1946) [Existentialism and Humanism (1948)].

It was Sartre's stories and novels that brought him widespread public acclaim, especially for *La Nausée* (1938) [Nausea (1949)], *Le Mur* (1939) [The Wall and Other Stories (1948)], *Les Chemins de la liberté* [The Roads to Freedom]: volume 1, *L'Age de raison* (1945) [The Age of Reason (1947)], volume 2, *Le Sursis* (1945) [The Reprieve (1947)], and volume 3, *La Mort dans l'âme* (1949) [Iron in the Soul (1950), translated in the U.S. as Troubled Sleep (1951)]. His literary criticisms and political writings included *Réflexions sur la question juive* (1946) [Portrait of the Anti-Semite (1948)], *Baudelaire* (1947) [Baudelaire (1949)], *Saint Genet, comédien et martyr* (1952) [Saint Genet: Actor and Martyr (1963)], *Situations*, vols. 1–10 (1947–1976), and *L'Idiot de la famille* (1972) [The Family Idiot: Gustave Flaubert, 1821–1857 (1981–1989)]. His theatrical works proved even more popular: *Les Mouches* (1943) [The Flies (1963)], *Huis clos* (1945) [No Exit (1946)], *La Putain respectueuse* (1946) [The Respectful Prostitute (1949)], *Les Mains sales* (1948) [Dirty Hands (1949)], and *Le Diable et le bon dieu* (1951) [Lucifer and the Lord (1953)].

Eager to address the complex issues of his day, Sartre was an intensely committed political activist until the end of his life (he participated in the Russell Tribunal, refused the Nobel Prize for Literature in 1964, and took over the management of the publications *La Cause du peuple* and, later, *Libération*). He died in Paris on April 15, 1980.

For more information, readers are referred to the biography by Annie Cohen-Solal, *Sartre: A Life*, translated by Anna Cancogni (New York: Pantheon, 1987).

Index